EPIC BOOKS AND CAFE
PRESENTS

American Heritage

Prophecy Series

The Destiny Of A Nation From
A Kingdom Perspective

PAULA MATTHEWS

SL
Spirit & Life
Publications^{SM}

EPIC Books And Cafe Presents

American Heritage Prophecy Series

"Scripture taken from The Message. Copyright © 1993, 1994, 1995, 1996, 2000, 2001, 2002. Used by permission of NavPress Publishing Group."

Unless otherwise noted all scripture is taken from
The Holy Bible
King James Version

Published by
Spirit & Life Publications℠
Los Angeles

Printed in the United States
ISBN: 978-0-9851172-8-3

Honor All People,
Love The Brethren,
Fear God,
Honor The King

I Peter 2:17 (KJV)

CONTENTS

CONTENTS

AUTHOR'S NOTE

On The Subject Of Love, Honor And Truth

The Bible has much to say about honor, and yet honor seems to be somewhat absent in our day. Cynicism and skepticism are the norm, even in the church. Americans are focused more on their own de-sires to be esteemed and honored; but true honor only comes when we yield to the wisdom of God. Proverbs says that when we esteem God's wisdom and honor him, we will receive both riches and honor. King Solomon was the greatest example of this truth. As the son and successor of his father David, he could have asked God for wealth and revenge against his enemies, but he didn't. Solomon asked for wisdom and understanding to rule over God's people. Because his heart was set upon honoring God in his dealings with the people, God gave Solomon not only wisdom and understanding, but he also gave him wealth, riches and honor. The Bible mentions numerous promises for those who choose to live honorable before God and man. These promises include long life, protection from enemies, answered prayer, prosperity and peace on earth.

Jesus criticized the church of his day and he called them hypocrites. He said that they honored God with their lips, but their hearts were far from him (Mark 7:6-9,13). He also accused them of worshipping God in vain because they reject the commandments of God to teach the commandments of men. They also practiced religion traditions that rendered the word of God of no effect. The importance of living honorable was a common topic in the teachings of the first apostles. The Apostle Paul told believers to honor their relationships with one an-other as if relating to God. He admonishes us to do nothing out of self ambition and pride, but to esteem God and others above ourselves. He even gave us an incentive to do so. Paul said that whatever good we do for one another, the Lord would make happen for us; and yet American Christians seem far removed from the concept of honoring and esteeming God and others. Jesus came to return us to love and honor. He did so by providing us with truth and grace. God's word is truth and his Holy Spirit imparts the grace that enables us to walk in that truth. Therefore, Jesus reduced the whole duty of men into two commandments: *Love God with all your heart, your mind and strength, and Love your neighbor as you love yourself.*

We love ourselves, but we have yet to perfect our love for God or for our fellow man. So, where did we go wrong in America? The church says that America has strayed from God, but the Spirit of God blames the church for what has happened in our nation. He says that a spirit of rebellion has fallen upon our nation because the church is in rebellion against God. That is according to God's kingdom order. It is also the reason we must return to honoring God and honoring one another. God's kingdom has a designated order of command and authority. Some would call it a military chain of command, but it's deeper than that. It is God's kingdom chain of accountability. The commands may come down in descending order, but the accountability comes back to each of us in ascending order. Jesus left the church as a spiritual overseer of the world. This is how God established the world at creation. The church is commanded to pick up the battalion where Adam dropped it.

Adam was given dominion over this earth, but when he chose to do his own thing he was cursed and thrown out of the Garden of Eden. One man's curse caused all the earth and its inhabitants to be cursed as well. Adam was charged with sinning against God even though he tried to blame it all on Eve; and there are preachers today who in their ignorance concerning God's order still blame Eve and all women for the issues of the world. The Spirit of God tells a different story. Adam was given the highest level of authority over the earth. God gave Adam direct commands. Eve was under Adam's commanded, therefore she got her orders from Adam. It was his responsibility to see that she obeyed, but that's not what happened. The Bible records that Eve was deceived by the serpent, but what about Adam? He deliberately sinned against God. Adam set Eve up to take the fall. God told him that if he disobeyed and ate from the forbidden tree, he would surely die. She may have been deceived, but Adam was deceitful. Even though he may have been unaware of how the consequences would play out, Adam knew exactly what he was doing,. Rather than taking responsibility for his own actions, Adam placed the blame on the woman.

In the eyes of God, the church is doing the same thing in America. The church is blaming Americans for sins that could have been avoided if the church had done it's job in obedience to God. Like Adam, the church received direct commands from God, but also like Adam the church has another agenda in mind. God's plan is not the church's plan. This is willful rebellion. This is the same sin that Adam committed in the garden. Similarly the cursed church has caused America to also live under a curse. There are many in the American church who have deceived themselves into believing that since Jesus left them in charge, they can do whatever they please. This is not true. Jesus left us with an example of how to live with our fellow man. They have just chosen not to follow his example. Jesus was moved with love and compassion for people. He hated religion, deceit and anything that oppressed people. He was anointed with the Holy Ghost and with fire. He went about doing good and healing all who were oppressed by the devil (Acts 10:38). Jesus commanded us to do as he did. Too many Christians go about using God's word as a rod of abuse and oppression that condemns men to death. Jesus did not come to condemn the world. He came that we might have abundant life on this earth. It is not God's will that any man should die, but that all should come to the knowledge of the truth. The kingdom of God is not about rules, it's about righteousness, peace and joy in the Holy Ghost.

The Lord has commanded me to write and publish this book of prophecy. A prophecy is any message spoken or revealed by the Holy Spirit to the hearts of men on earth. Prophecies can pertain to a current issue and/ or a future promise from God to his people. Spirit-filled believers receive prophetic messages from the Holy Spirit concerning their specific assignments. They also receive prophetic messages concerning their personal, professional and church family relationships. These messages come in the form of instructions or directive information. They can also be corrective. The information received may prevent one from danger or from incurring the wrath of God in a particular situation. Although any believer can receive prophecies, only the prophet is ordained by God to declare such messages for the perfection and maturing of the Body of Christ.

The Bible is a book of prophecies written by the prophets of old. The major difference is that the prophecies in this book were given to me by the Holy Spirit about life in America. These prophecies do not replace what is in the Bible, but they do clarify God's plan and purpose for the church and the citizens of our nation. God's promise to his people is that every word of prophecy (both that which is written in the Bible and that which is spoken to the hearts of men) must come to pass before heaven and earth pass away. The question then becomes that of timing. When will these things come to pass? Jesus said that it is not for us to know

13

the times and seasons that only God has determined for his knowledge. Instead, our focus should be on doing the assignment he gave each of us to do while looking for the signs of those seasons. It is the job of the prophet to announce the seasons and to declare the ways of God's spirit in this earth. When the prophet speaks it should give credence to, and confirmation for every individual word of prophecy spoken to each of us by the Holy Spirit. The word from the prophet should also confirm what God has already stated in the Bible. Again, only God knows the exact timing, but the prophetic word should always motivate God's people to make preparations to align themselves to fulfill that which is good, acceptable and perfect in His sight.

The spirit behind a true word of prophecy will always direct one's attention to the testimony of Jesus Christ and what was accomplished at the cross. Prophecy leads to a greater understanding of God's plan for men as it relates to the redemption and restoration work of the cross. This is true for the individual, the church and for anyone who receives a prophetic word. Prophecy should show how God's plan for the individual or entity fits into the greater scheme of God's kingdom agenda. This is the true essence of all prophecy that comes from God, and so it shall be in the prophecies contained in this book. The only difference may be in the interpretation of known Bible scripture. The error most Christians make is in their human interpretation of spiritual matters. The Bible is both spiritual and prophetic in nature. Which means that true wisdom and understanding of the prophetic word can only be revealed by the Holy Spirit. Now, I am about to say something that may be difficult for religious ears to hear, but here it is. Just because a verse is in the Bible doesn't make it true in the situation you may be experiencing at a specific moment in time.

In Matthew Chapter 4, it says that Jesus was led into the wilderness by the Holy Spirit to be tempted by Satan. Do you remember how Satan tempted Jesus? He used the Bible. Satan knows the Bible and he attempted to use it against Jesus. Obviously knowing what was written was not enough for Jesus to win against Satan, and neither is it enough for Christians in our day. Jesus was led by the Holy Spirit in this battle. Jesus' actions and his words came directly from the Holy Spirit. Jesus had the written scriptures, but he lived his life by walking in the spirit. Years ago, the Lord shared his heart on this matter. He told me that Jesus could not have survived on this earth without the Holy Spirit. We think

14

of Jesus as being the Son of God, who walked on this earth as God. This is not so. Although he was the Son of God, when Jesus left heaven and came to earth, he had to give up his heavenly status to walk as a man in this earth. Jesus walked in the full power of God not because of his status in heaven, but because of his earthly alignment with God the father and God the Holy Spirit. Jesus came to show us how we should live on earth if we want to manifest the same power from heaven. The Lord stressed that if Jesus had not been obedient to the Spirit of God, he too would have been lost in this earth. He said, *"If Jesus needed the Holy Spirit? What makes Christians think they don't need him to survive in this world?"*

Not only did the Holy Spirit speak these words to me, but he also took me through the Bible to read Jesus' own words on the matter. Jesus said that he did and said only what he saw his father do and what he heard his father speak. If Jesus was on earth and God was in heaven how could he see or hear his father speak? Jesus was connected to God by the Holy Spirit. You may remember that his mother Mary was a virgin at his conception. The Holy Spirit came upon her and she conceived. Jesus was born of the Spirit. When he died and resurrected, that same Holy Spirit became available to every born again human on earth. Jesus came to earth to show us how to *"live as human beings genetically altered by the Holy Spirit."* That is exactly what he was. He was born as a man but genetically altered in his human spirit. This same process happens when one becomes born again. Therefore we, as born again men can walk as Jesus walked on earth. As he is, so are we in this world. The Holy Spirit is in us. We need only to train our hearts and minds to see and hear what the spirit is saying at all times.

How many times did Jesus say to his followers, he that has ears to hear let him hear? Everyone has ears, but not all can hear what the spirit is speaking. Even with the Holy Spirit within us, the born again believer has to make a conscious and deliberate choice to have an ear that is open to the spirit, and a heart that is willing to be obedient. In America there are many voices vying for our attention. We tune in to what we want to hear. If there is something that we don't like, we tune our ears to another voice and another message. The same is true with God's word. Sometimes God's word is hard to hear because it requires us to change our minds and to change our direction in life.

Throughout the Bible, you will find words like: *hearken, be attentive, give ear, take heed, to wake, watch or be watchful, be sober, be vigilante*. These and similar words appear throughout the gospels and the letters to the churches. In the book of Revelation alone, it is written five times, *"He that hath an ear, let him hear what the Spirit saith unto the churches."* Repeatedly, God is trying to get his people to not only hear, but to pay attention to what his spirit is saying, and yet Christians still rebel against the voice of God. It is particularly an issue with Americans who feel they have a right to live anyway they choose. They rebel against God's word anytime its interferes with their lifestyle. There is a belief in our nation that God is mean and controlling, and all he wants to do is curtail our fun. This is far from the truth. In fact one truly has never known either fun or a meaningful life until he or she lets the Holy Spirit lead. You will find yourself on an adventure of a lifetime. We should always hear and obey God because he knows the traps and snares the enemy has set for our lives.

God understands that although he calls us and anoints us for his service, Satan also dispatches his demons to stop us at every turn. God's word assures us that we will have fun and adventure without penalty and disaster, and if the enemy snare is in your midst, your obedience will cause the trap to backfire on the one who set it. Danger can come, but our obedience will keep it from harming us. Psalm 91:7 says that *"A thousand shall fall at thy side, and ten thousand at thy right hand; [but] it shall not come nigh thee."* People could be dropping like flies around us, but when we obey God's word, nothing will not touch us. This is why our eyes should always be open and our ears should be attentive to what the spirit is saying. There is a level of truth and understanding that can only be revealed by the Holy Spirit. This is how Jesus lived on earth. This is also how God expects each of us to live on a daily basis; not in the futility of our human understanding, but in the power of his Holy Spirit.

The reason religious people use the Bible to hurt others is because they don't have ears to hear what the spirit is saying. They are not connected to the Holy Spirit; the one who reveals the heart and mind of God. They may know the words of the Bible, but the Spirit of Truth (who is the Holy Spirit) is not leading them into all of the truth. So often these same people have no idea that they are speaking wrong words, at the wrong time and with the wrong spirit.

Religious people are usually not interested in seeking truth, they are more concern about becoming God's authority in another person's life. Some are just plain ignorant about God's ways, others desire to control and manipulate weak-minded souls. Some prophecies contained in this book may offend religious minds who are sticklers for enforcing the law of God. Know this. In God's kingdom the greatest law in any situation will always be that of love; loving God and loving others. The Spirit of God has expressed to me that he has a *"Special Grace"* that he extends to unbelievers. This should be common knowledge for every believer. If we think about what we did before coming to Jesus. There were many times God should have passed judgment against us, but he chose not to do so. Again, this type of wisdom can only be revealed if the Holy Spirit is leading us in each situation. On the other hand, God is merciful to all, but he will not always strive with men who continually rebel against his will. There are some prophetic messages in this book that may speak of God's judgment. Harsh judgment is inevitable for God's people who continually block the way of the kingdom and who place stumbling blocks in the way of men who are seeking to do God's will. It is the responsibility of the prophet to warn people and exhort them to change before judgment falls upon their lives.

Although the words, love and honor may not appear in every prophecy, please know that this is the intent of every word. In God's kingdom the prophets are the royal court announcers. We speak whatever God declares over his kingdom and it's people. Don't think that the prophet's duties end there. For every word God has me speak, I spend hours, days and weeks in prayer that his people would obey so that God's will can be done. The Holy Spirit often awakens me out sleep. He interrupts my days and nights beckoning me to pray that his people would return their hearts to him in obedience. I pray that each of you receive this book in the spirit in which it has been prepared for you. God wants his people to strengthen their weak hands and feeble knees so that his glory may be seen upon them. This can only be done if we are strong in the Lord and in the power of his might, not in that which is of our own strength. A return to love and honor would allow God's power to work great exploits on our behalf. This is the testimony of Jesus' resurrection power that will also transform the world from darkness to light.

The prophetic words in this book typed in *"**Bold Italic Quotes.**"* They are also organized in four main categories: 1) prophecies for America, 2) prophecies for the church, 3) prophecies about fearing God, and 4) prophecies concerning the President of the United States. We have also included key scripture references so that truth is presented in the mouths of two or three witnesses. Jesus said that you will know the truth and it would make you free. God's word is truth. The Holy Spirit is called the *Spirit of Truth.* He is responsible for leading us into all the truth about life. Not truth as man sees it, but the truth of God that give us hope and leads to prosperity.

The Holy Spirit speaks the truth of God's word to the hearts of men. When we obey that truth, we also find freedom. Wherever the Spirit is Lord, there is both liberty and freedom. Truth, when spoken in love, also purifies the hearts and minds of men. Truth is something that yearns to be demonstrated as a loving example for all men to follow. God's truth is his wisdom for our daily lives that is designed to bring us back to our wealthy place in him. Why shouldn't this be the case? God is love, and if he and his word are the same that means his word (truth) is an expression of that love; and when we obey that word of truth we also express our love and honor for God.

When love and honor flows from our hearts to God, it will then flow out to our fellow man and open all the channels of this life to receive the abundance of God's wealth and resources from heaven. The Holy Spirit spoke these transforming words of truth to me during prayer, ***"The Kingdom of God has always been about changing the lives of human beings by ridding the earth of hunger, sickness, disease, poverty and human degradation. This is Christianity. It's not a religion. It's a way of living (kingdom living); a way of loving and sharing with our fellow man."***

INTRODUCTION

Why It Had To Be Jesus

The Holy Spirit told me that there was about to be *"A Restoration of An Ancient Kingdom Dynasty"* in the earth. It didn't take me long to figure this one out, because I had heard this same prophetic word form the Lord a couple of years ago. The word restoration implies that this dynasty had previously existed at an earlier point in time. The dynasty referred to in this prophecy is the original dynasty that began when God created Adam and placed him in the Garden of Eden. It was God's plan for man to rule on earth just like God ruled from heaven. Even after Adam sinned and he and Eve were banished from the garden, it was always God's plan to restore man to his place of ruling and reigning on earth. Jesus came to earth to restore this plan for men. The Old Testament prophets spoke about God creating his kingdom in the earth. Jesus was the prophesied Messiah who would reign over God's kingdom.

Religion and human suppositions muddled the interpretation of God's plan for men. Abraham was seeking for a city whose builder and maker was God. The Jews are looking for the rebuilding of the temple and their Messiah to rule on earth. Christians are looking for Jesus to break through the skies where we all would be caught up together with him and go to heaven. Are they all wrong? In the eyes of God, they are all right in what they speak, but how it will manifest is totally in God's hands. God's thoughts and his ways are much higher than ours. Sometimes God has to start with what we know and lead us in baby steps to his grand design. The problem with prophecy is that men think they know God's plan and they try to bring it to pass with their human efforts. It cannot be done. Prophecy only comes to pass as we follow the voice of God in our daily lives.

When the Holy Spirit spoke to me about this introduction he directed me to the first two chapters of Genesis and the last two chapters in the book of Revelation. He said that if we had any doubt about God's plan for man on earth, these chapters would highlight the general ideas that human beings should note. First and foremost, there is a city that will descend from heaven and remain on the earth. It is called the New Jerusalem. Like Eden this city has rivers of living waters and in its center there is the tree of life. This is a city created for human habitation and rulership under the domain of God. There will be a vast amount of wealth and abundance in this city just like there was in Eden. Like Eden, there will be no sickness, dying or crying in the New Jerusalem. Also the evil serpent who beguiled Eve will be no more. Death, Hell and all those who were not in the Book of Life would have already been swallowed up in the Lake of Fire.

So who are the inhabitants of this great city? Are they Christians? Are they Jews? Here is where things get real interesting. In this New Jerusalem there will be people from every nation, every tongue and every tribe. All of humanity will be there; every people group will be represented in this new city. Here is why. When God created Adam, he blessed him by saying, Be fruitful, and multiply, and replenish the earth, and subdue it: and have dominion (Genesis 1:28). All nations, tongues and tribes were destined to come from the loins of Adam as a righteous seed. When Adam fell, the seed became corrupted in his curse, and man could no longer rule under God's authority in this earth. Men have been ruling, but it has been under the power of the kingdom of darkness. Jesus came to break the curse and to restore men to their righteous standing, not so they could go to heaven, but so they could take their rightful inheritance and rule on this earth.

You might be wondering how it is possible for men to rule under God's authority on earth while living amongst those in the kingdom of darkness. It takes an abundance of God's grace and his free gift of righteousness that comes through receiving Jesus Christ as Lord and Savior. The major objective for God's Kingdom has always been restoration. Jesus came to do more than take away the curse and the sin that resulted from Adam's sin. He came to seek and save that which was lost in the darkness of this world. Jesus had restoration on his mind. He said that he came to give us life and life more abundantly. He wasn't talking about life in heaven. Jesus was talking about abundant life here on earth. Jesus came to show us how we could be the light in the midst of great darkness. The darkness of this world is the pain and suffering and death that has reigned in the earth under Adam's curse. Jesus came preaching and demonstrating the power of God's kingdom over poverty, sickness, disease, death and over all the power the curse. Religion would have you believe that we are powerless over the evil of this earth, but that is not the message that Jesus taught.

Jesus not only taught about the power of the kingdom, but when he resurrected from the grave, he declared that all power in heaven and in the earth belonged to him. He then turned that power over to his followers and commanded them to go into all the world preaching and demonstrating the gospel of the kingdom. Jesus said that these signs would follow those who believed: *"In my name shall they cast out devils; they shall speak with new tongues; They shall take up serpents; and if they drink any deadly thing, it shall not hurt them; they shall lay hands on the sick, and they shall recover* (Mark 16:17-18). *"*

As mentioned earlier, the Jews were anticipating that their Messiah would come and set up his kingdom on the earth. When Jesus claimed to be the Messiah and claimed that his kingdom was not of this world, it confused many Jews. Some asked the whereabouts of his kingdom. Jesus said that it was inside of them and they labeled him a heretic. They knew the prophecies, but they didn't have the spirit to lead them to the lead them to the truth, so the church leaders of his day had him crucified as a blasphemer. Even after his resurrection there was still some confusion amongst the disciples. They were anticipating that Jesus was going set up his earthly kingdom at that time. Again, we have human beings trying to bring to pass prophecy without the Spirit of God. Jesus told them to forget about when the kingdom was coming to earth, but that they would receive power when the Holy Spirit was come upon them. Then they would have the power to become witnesses of his resurrection. Can you imagine their level of confusion. The disciples spent three years walking and talking with Jesus and yet they were still confused as to why he came to earth and why he resurrected. It wasn't until the Holy Spirit came on the day of Pentecost and fell upon each of them that they could begin to understand what was going on. Even today, the kingdom of God is shrouded in mysteries than can only be revealed and interpreted by the Holy Spirit.

So far we have learned that Jesus had to come to earth to restore us to righteousness. He also came to demonstrate the power of God's kingdom and prove that any human could do the same after being endued with power from the Holy Spirit. There is an even greater reason that Jesus came to earth. When the Lord explained this to me years ago, I was amazed at the genius of God. He took me through the Bible and showed how he was always in search of a people who would obey him so that they could receive the inheritance that Adam lost. He showed

21

me that after the flood, Noah and his sons were given the same promise and blessing that was given to Adam. They were also commissioned to go into all the earth to be fruitful and multiply into nations of righteous people who would be obedient to God. Noah's son Shem was the only one who kept the promise. Abraham was a descendant of Shem, which qualified him to receive the inheritance. Abraham also had the promise of being the father of many nations even when he was too old to conceive a child. God brought the prophecy to pass, but he also let Abraham know that his descendants would be enslaved for over four hundred years before they could be the nation he promised. And so it was.

Moses was sent to free the descendants of Abraham out of bondage in Egypt to fulfill the covenant promise. The promise was to make them a nation, but they had been enslaved in darkness for so long that God had to retrain them in the ways of righteousness. God gave Moses the Ten Commandments to demonstrate what was considered sin in God's kingdom. It was just a tiny baby step to show the people God's way of righteousness, but instead of moving closer to God, the Jews became a nation deeply steeped in religious laws and doctrines that had very little to do with God's plan for their lives. God sent Jesus to the Jews to get them back on track with God's plan for his kingdom. He spoke about God's fatherly love for them, and the people could not understand this way of thinking. To them God was a lawgiver and a judge who ruled by death and fire. When Jesus began demonstrating the grace of God's kingdom toward sinners, church leaders were offended and accused him of violating the laws of Moses. Their minds were closed to the idea that God would every extend love, mercy or grace to any human.

When Jesus' message was rejected by the Jews, Jesus commanded the disciples to take the message to the world. In fact, the world had heard the message once from Adam after the fall, and again when Noah and his sons repopulated the earth. The message of the kingdom has always been intended for all people of the earth. That was God's original command to Adam and Noah, and it was Jesus' command to the church. Unfortunately, the church in America has fallen into the same religious trap that distracted the ancient Jews. Although they received the message of the salvation for themselves, many have become hoarders of the same message that Jesus commanded them to share with the world. Why won't they share the message? The Holy Spirit said that the church in America has become like Jonah who refused to go to Nineveh to spare them from the wrath of God. Jonah felt that the people of Nineveh were too sinful to be awarded the grace of God. Likewise, many in the Christian church in America have deemed the people of our nation unworthy to be saved. So they have refused to obey God for the benefit of this nation.

Just as the Jews made a clear division between themselves and gentiles, many Christians have made a similar line separating themselves from non-believers. Jesus told us to love others as we love ourselves, but many Christians prefer to condemn the nation and reserve a place in God's kingdom only for those who think, act and look like them. This is not the way of God's kingdom. Jesus had to take the message out of the hands of the disobedient and commission others who would be faithful to carry out God's plan for men on earth. In God's Kingdom men are no longer divided by religion such as Jew or Gentile. Neither are we divided as slave or free, male or female, Black, White, Brown, Yellow or Red Man; in God's Kingdom we are ONE NEW MAN, one new Adam, the Body of Christ, united as one Body and One Spirit, in communion under one Lord, one faith, one baptism; one God and Father of all. The family of God united both in heaven and in earth, made up of people from every nation, tribe and tongue, subject to the peace and blessings of God unto ETERNAL LIFE FOREVER. This is the message of the Gospel of the Kingdom of God. This was the picture of the earth that God gave Adam at creation, it is also the picture of God's kingdom in the book of Revelation. There will be no more religion, or temples or even Sabbath days. The Bible says that there will be no need for those things because God and his Son Jesus will be our temple and we will worship them for all eternity. This is exactly how it was in Eden. Adam and Eve had no need for religion, they had God walking and talking with them in the garden.

This is eternal life as God designed it from the foundation of the world. It began with Adam and ended with Jesus. Today it is available to anyone who is willing to totally surrender his life to Jesus and perform mighty acts of God in defense of the suffering masses; to comfort all who mourn by giving them the good news of God's Kingdom: with man it may be impossible, but with God All Things are Possible!

HONOR ALL PEOPLE

God ordained Christians to be the light of the world to illuminate the truth. We are the salt of the earth because we are called to preserve that which is good and to be a healing agent for those who are weary. Salt adds a flavor that makes food more palatable and enjoyable, and so should be the life of a Christian in the midst of those who don't know our Lord. Jesus said that they should see our good works and glorify our father which is in heaven (Matthew 5:16).

The Apostle Peter takes the discussion of honor to yet another level. He encourages the church to be to careful honor all men, even if it means suffering for doing and standing for what is good. When the Lord began talking to me about this section, there was disappointment in the heart of the father because his people have failed to see the honor in suffering for what is good. Although Jesus gave us the example to follow, the Church in America seems not to understand this concept at all. One of the reasons for this has to do with the proliferation of free, yet dishonorable speech and verbal retaliation that flows through the social media culture. Americans fight for their right to freedom of speech and yet Christians are warned that they will be judged by every word they speak. By our words we will be justified and by our words we will be condemned (Matthew 12:37). Social media is filled with idle words that mock, ridicule, and slander the lives of some many innocent people. It may be legal, but Christians will be judged for every idle word they speak.

Christians are also commanded to speak the truth in love, but they have proven to be just as dishonorable in what they say about unbelievers and about those who are in authority over our nation. Many times, when they do speak the truth as it appears in the Bible, it is spoken in hatred. It is done as a political and religious deception that maligns a group or particular thought that disagrees with their doctrine. We forget that there were just as many unjust laws, perverted and sinful people in Jesus' day. If we look at the example Jesus demonstrated while on the earth, he never spoke evil about sinners or about the rulers of their nation. In fact, he did just the opposite. He gave honor to whom honor was due. Now, Jesus often gave rebuke to whom it was due, and most times it was given to the leaders of the church who were hypocrites and lawbreakers themselves.

Even when he was unjustly charged and executed as a criminal by the ancient Roman government, Jesus never said a word to either defend himself or to condemn his executioners. They beat him to a pulp. They put a crown of thorns on his head and spat on him. Then they made him carry a heavy cross to the top of a mountain side where they nailed him to the cross. They did all of this to Jesus and yet he never said a word; and before he died he said, *"Father forgive them for they know not what they do."*

Many readers would say, that was Jesus. He was the son of God. He didn't have to put up with the world that we know today. Well, hold on a moment. Doesn't it say in Hebrews 4:15 that Jesus was tempted in all ways as we are, and yet he lived on earth without sin? Why did he do this? Think about it. Jesus came to earth and experienced every kind of relationship issue that we now face on earth, minus the obvious techno-logical and cultural differences. People are people. There has not be a generation of humans on the face of this earth that has experience any more temptations that Jesus did himself. This is why God appointed him as our high priest. He has compassion for our earthly condition and the Holy Spirit relays to our spirits the way of escape for sin. So, if we are being led by the Holy Spirit, we will know what to speak and when to speak it; and our manner of speech will convey love, truth and honor to the hearer. Unfortunately many Christians exercise their right to speak and never follow the example that Jesus left us. Jesus said that he only did and only said what his father did and said. It was the Holy Spirit that led Jesus to speak and act as the spirit willed. Jesus' mouth never led him to sin against God. It is the desire of the father that the same be said of Christians in America. Our mouths are to be used to bless and not to curse. We are to speak life and not death. We are to draw sinners to our Lord by our manner of speech and our behavior, even if it means keeping our mouth shut before men and opening our mouths and hearts before God in prayer for direction.

There is no free speech in the Kingdom of God. We are taught that evil communications corrupt good manners. Christians are not to pat-tern themselves after the mockers and scorners in this world. We are not to follow after wicked advice like those that don't know God . . . and yet many Christians suffer and perish because they reject the wisdom and government of God in these areas, in lieu of the freedoms afforded un-der the United States Constitution. This is not saying that there is any wrong with our constitution, but God requires exemplary demonstration of his government in the lives of the members of the church. We are to be the example of a new and living way that prosperous and honors all men. Christians practice at spewing the letter of God's law without heavenly guidance. We have a new covenant and although it is written, it is administered by the spirit. When we use the written word without the spirit, it brings death to the hearer. When led by the spirit, the same word would become a healing balm to those who are weary. Knowing when and how to speak requires a listening ear and an obedient heart.

The Apostle Peter had much to say about honoring all people. He teaches us how to honor our loved ones as well as unbelievers. His first word of advice is for believers to lay aside all malice, deceit, hypocrisy, envy and all evil speaking. Instead, he urges us to desire the pure word of God so that we can grow to maturity in the faith. The Apostle Paul tells us to do everything in a way that esteems other higher than ourselves. Peter takes it a step further by telling us to submit to one another even to the point of suffering in silence like Jesus did on the cross. In this chapter we will look at how one can fulfill such a strenuous requirement in our homes, on the job and with all men.

Honoring Our Parents And Elders

According to Genesis 1:12, God created every living thing to yield seeds according to its own kind. This means that every human is a seed from someone else's harvest. Have you ever seen a seedling of a plant? It is connected firmly to a vine, that is connected to a branch of a tree or a shrub. Nothing in this existence sustains life on its own. We are all connected to each other and to our past. Which means that our conduct today will determine how we connect to future generations on this earth. When we dishonor our parents and elders, we cut ourselves loose from the vine of life that connects us. A seedling cut off from the vine will surely die. Therefore, we are commanded to honor our parents so that we can prosper and live long on this earth. Many of us could begin to live fruitful and honorable lives just by honoring those who came before us. No matter how we feel about our parents or how we were raised, each of us owes a debt of gratitude and honor to those who gave us life; especially in a culture where abortion is heavily promoted as a woman's choice. The fact that your parents made a choice to give birth is proof that there are still people who honor God's command to multiply their seed in this earth. Whether or not they produced a fruitful harvest from that seed is another issue. God has placed within this earth a series of spiritual laws that determine the course of every human decision in life. These laws connect every generation of human life to previous generations. That is why children are called *offspring* and *descendants*. They are the result of a specific ancestry that was handed down to them.

It is interesting that people descend and not ascend in their ancestry. Descending implies that the later generation is greater than those that which follows, it. In Bible times, that was definitely true. When God blessed a man, it was to him and his future generations. The first of such blessings was recorded in Genesis. The promise of dominion, abundance and prosperity was given to God's son Adam and he was to propagate this blessing throughout all generations of humans on the earth. When Adam sinned in the Garden of Eden, something radically changed. He cut himself loose from the vine of life in heaven and death came into the earth. Instead of the blessing being propagated, death and the curse was passed on to all generations of humans on this earth. Which brings us to another reason one should honor his or her parents. Every result we have obtained in this life; whether good or bad, is a result the seeds that were sown by us, and on our behalf by our parents, and by their parents, and by the parents who went before them (Galatians 6:7). This is a spiritual law that exits in the earth. It's the law of Seedtime and Harvest. It works the same for human culture as it does for agriculture. If we want better results, we have to sow seeds that will produce better results. God's word is incorruptible seed (I Peter 1:23) that will grow and flourish if we follow the instructions.

How we honor our parents also reflects how we honor God. One of the reasons many people have difficulty accepting God as father is because they have such a poor image of their earthly father. Most of us tend to judge all fathers by the one that failed (or exceeded) *our expectations*. The Bible repeatedly refers to God as a good father who wants only the best for his children, but if your earthly father was a bad father, you may not want to hear that God wants to be your father. The relation-ship with our earthly fathers must be reconciled before we are able to fully receive what God has for our lives. It all begins with forgiveness. Parents learn to parent from their parents. Nobody is perfect, and yet almost every child will grow up with some complaint about how they were raised. In God's kingdom how you were raised should not stop his plan for your life. Everyone born after Adam, was born under the curse. We all came to this earth bearing bad crops from the bad seeds our forefathers have sown. God took all of this into account before your parents even thought about getting together. God knows our flaws and shortcomings, and still he loves us and has a good plan for our lives (Jeremiah 29:11).

So how does one get pass their past and obtain the blessing of God? Again, it begins with forgiveness. Your parents did the best they could. I may be the author of this book, but I know first hand what it's like to be in a dysfunctional family. I had to forgive my parents, and when I did, the Lord offered to be my father. I was in high school at the time. He said that neither of my parents could not love me the way they should because they had never experienced love. They could not give me some-thing they never had. On the other hand, no one knows about love more than God, because God is love (I John 4:8). When he showers you with his love it is like nothing any human could ever do for you. Now that I am older, I see the change in my parents. They have even admitted that they didn't know what they were doing way back then. The Lord told me recently that there was a family inheritance blessing that my dad never obtained, but as an obedient child of God, I have full access to this inheritance. A seedling cut off from the vine will die, unless it is rooted and grounded in fertile soil. When I began to be rooted and grounded in the love of God, I learned how to honor my parents. It was then that I began living life according to God's promise. Years later, the Lord would share that my dad's sole purpose was to get me born into this earth. Once I was here, it was up to me to find my purpose and make life better for future generations. That is exactly what Jesus did by coming to this earth. He regained the inheritance that Adam lost. Now, all who receive Jesus as Lord, have become heirs to that same inheritance. So, even if your natural parents didn't leave a godly inheritance, you can be born again into the family of God and become a partaker of Abraham's blessings; and a joint heir with Jesus of all that belongs to God, both in heaven and in this earth.

Key Scripture References

Genesis 17:1-2,7
And when Abram was ninety years old and nine, the LORD appeared to Abram, and said unto him, I [am] the Almighty God; walk before me, and be thou perfect. And I will make my covenant between me and thee, and will multiply thee exceedingly. And I will establish my covenant between me and thee and thy seed after thee in their generations for an everlasting covenant, to be a God unto thee, and to thy seed after thee.

Exodus 20:12
Honour thy father and thy mother: that thy days may be long upon the land which the LORD thy God giveth thee.

God-Willed Not Self-Willed

In the matter of honoring all men, God expects believers to be led by the spirit, to full His will and not their own in this life. The salvation experience results in a new species of god/human where the heart, mind and spirit of God is deposited within the heart of a man or woman who believes that Jesus is Lord. The Apostle Paul said that since we are new creatures, all things new and all things are of God. He said that was the purpose behind Jesus' death and resurrection, so that all who receive him should no longer live for themselves, but for him who died and rose again for them (II Corinthians 5:14-18). He called believers to the ministry of reconciliation, where they would be ambassadors of Christ. Ambassadors represent their home country on foreign soil. The same is true of the ambassador for Christ. Your conduct and lifestyle should represent the interest of God's Kingdom. An ambassador's job is to educate those of the host nation about the way of his or her home nation. It's the highest ranking Public Relations representative of any nation. The ambassador is also expected to develop key economic, cultural and scientific relationship between the two nations. Unfortunately, many religions create more terror for the nations than they do diplomacy. Religion produces fear and oppression whereas in Christianity, God is love (I John 4:8).

Where the Spirit is Lord, there is freedom (II Corinthians 3:17). It would seem that many people, especially Christians, would want this freedom, but it is not so. In this world, people succeed in life by placing bonds of oppression on people. Whether it is an evil employer or a dysfunctional church or a home where domestic violence is the norm, oppression is a way of life for many people. Even look at American politics. People fight over gun control, over government spending, over abortion and gay marriage. Take a moment to step away from the issues and look at the tactics being used. Fear tactics. Each side seems to be using fear to make their point; fear of possible disaster or fear of retaliation. This is even how the church operates. It uses fear and retaliation to demonstrate the gospel of Jesus Christ. The gospel is supposed to be good news, but you wouldn't know it by the way many in the church react to the world around them.

The prophet Isaiah said that if we are established in God's righteousness we would be free from oppression because we would not fear (Isaiah 54:14). Fear brings oppression and terror upon a people. God did not give us the spirit of fear; He gave us power, love and a sound mind (II Timothy 1:7); he gave us the power of the kingdom, the love of the father and the mind of Christ.

The Spirit of the Lord calls his people in America *"Self-Willed. They would rather be right in their own eyes than to be righteous in God's eyes."* The Bible has multiple scriptures warning us against everyone doing what is right in their own eyes. Without godly leadership, men covet and strive unlawfully with one another. They speak evil against one another and devise schemes upon their beds that they intend to carry out in the daylight hours. We're not just talking about the world, but also the church. The Lord wanted me to remind his people that there are six things he hates (Proverbs 6:16-19). Yes, seven are an abomination to Him: A proud look, A lying tongue, Hands that shed innocent blood, A heart that devises wicked plans, Feet that are swift in running to evil, A false witness who speaks lies, And one who sows discord among brethren.

In our main text of I Peter Chapter 2, Peter exhorts believers to live such good lives among nonbelievers that they accuse us of doing wrong. Don't try to justify yourselves by your words, let your good works defend you and these same people will glorify God on the day of visitation. Now, if you are being accuse because you are doing wrong, you have no defense in Christ. Repent and turn that thing around. Be an example of righteousness for others to follow.

The Lord says that if our nation is to turn around and be steered in the righteous direction, someone has to lead the way. It has to begin in the church. This is indeed God's plan for every nation of this earth. When the righteous are in authority, the people of the nation will rejoice. This is why we need to be led by the Holy Spirit; so that in our patience we can possess our souls; staying in the love and peace of God no matter what is going on around us.

Key Scripture References

Psalm 1:1-3

Blessed [is] the man that walketh not in the counsel of the ungodly, nor standeth in the way of sinners, nor sitteth in the seat of the scornful. But his delight [is] in the law of the LORD; and in his law doth he meditate day and night. And he shall be like a tree planted by the rivers of water, that bringeth forth his fruit in his season; his leaf also shall not wither; and whatsoever he doeth shall prosper.

Isaiah 50:4-5

The Lord GOD hath given me the tongue of the learned, that I should know how to speak a word in season to [him that is] weary: he wakeneth morning by morning, he wakeneth mine ear to hear as the learned. The Lord GOD hath opened mine ear, and I was not rebellious, neither turned away back.

You can tell what someone values by listening to the words of his or her mouth concerning that thing. Life and death are in the power of the tongue and they that love it will eat the fruit thereof (Proverbs 18:21). If we value life, we speak words and display actions that also value life. The opposite is also true if we don't value life. Look at our youth, the seedlings in America. So many young people are very disrespectful and dishonorable in both their words and deeds. The media promotes a hip-hop culture of outlaws that brag about gaining respect from their peers by dishonor, murder and intimidation. God calls this generation *"Lost!"* The sad thing about it, they don't know they are lost, because the money keeps rolling in the more they degrade themselves. Talk about negative reinforcement, these youth are recruiting others to follow their example just to get paid; and so often the end of that road leads to death; and no one seems to care. This is a curse that has been allowed to perpetuate throughout our nation and rather than intervene, *"The church has thrown this generation out with the trash."*

It's not all the fault of the youth because the Bible says if you train a child up in the way he or she should go, when they are older they won't depart from it. So what happened with the parents? According to the Lord, *"Americans don't value human life."* Even though this seems like a strong prophetic statement, it would explain why guns, drugs, pornography, sex trafficking, domestic violence and abortion are in the forefront of our nation's social and political issues. All of these issues involve dishonoring the human body with sin and trespass; and they didn't just "crop up." Generations of Americans have sown seeds of dishonor within our culture that have produced this deplorable harvest. The Lord blames the church for not demonstrating to the world his love and compassion for the human race.

Some believe that America began coming apart at the seams when prayer was taken out of the schools. I submit to you that it actually began when fervent effectual prayer was taken out of the church, and the Holy Spirit was deemed unnecessary in the merging age of technology. Christianity lost significant influence in our culture when church pastors and leaders chose celebrity and shunned purity and truth; when mega churches brought in mega bucks and prosperity-seekers; and Christians accepted sin as the norm. Rather than being salt and light in a rebellious culture, the American church joined in the spiral of moral decline in our nation. So, is there hope for America? Yes!

The Lord says that the hope for America rests in the youth. The adults may have given up on seeing honor, justice and truth, but according to the Lord, the youth are secretly yearning for someone to take the lead. They are seeking honor, its just that their methods are twisted because they have not been properly taught by those who know and should value honor: the church. God gave the church his Son, his Spirit and his plan for the nations of the world. Unfortunately the American church has taken the lead in the rebellion by rejecting everything God gave them. As an obedient remnant in the church begins to return to God's plan and purpose for their lives, it will cause momentum to flow in the direction of honor once again for the nation and its people. It will begin when believers start believing in God again. When they start speaking words of faith and not returning evil for evil with their adversaries; and they begin using their mouths for creating what God desires and not for tearing others down. When they start loving one another and operating in unity, only then will miraculous deliverance and prosperity abound, and the world will see it and glorify our God. Honor has to began at the house of God, and flow out to the public arena as a demonstration that God is who he said he is, and that Jesus Christ is lord of all.

Key Scripture References

I Peter 3:10-12
For he that will love life, and see good days, let him refrain his tongue from evil, and his lips that they speak no guile: Let him eschew evil, and do good; let him seek peace, and ensue it. For the eyes of the Lord [are] over the righteous, and his ears [are open] unto their prayers: but the face of the Lord [is] against them that do evil.

LOVE THE BROTHERHOOD

In this section, we will discuss honor amongst the brethren. Jesus commanded that we love another as he loved us. Believers in Jesus Christ are called to be children of God; and if children then we should demonstrate the features and characteristics of our father. God is love. Therefore every believer should speak and act in love. We should be imitators of God by walking in love and honor towards one another. Love and honor requires that we also submit one to another in reverence to God. Submitting to one another as God commands is the same as submitting to God himself. Submission is not just a command, but it is also for our protection.

Many Christians find themselves in sickness, disease and demonic control because they refuse to submit to God. James 4:7 says that if you want the devil to flee, you must first submit to God and his word. In and of ourselves, we have no power to wage a successful battle against demon spirits. That is why we are told to be strong in the Lord and in the power of his might. We are also commanded to put on *the whole armor of God* (Ephesians 6:10-12). Our warfare is not carnal (human). It's not against flesh and blood, but against principalities and spiritual powers that dominate the darkness of this world. Submission in this scripture is a Greek military term *hypotasso*[1] that refers to the ranking of military troops under a commander or leader. No one would walk into a battle without arming themselves, but that is exactly what it is like when believers refuse to submit to God's order of command.

Many people in America, including Christians treat the word submission as if it were a four letter word. Thanks to Adam's rebellion in the Garden of Eden, human beings naturally have a problem with submitting to authority. Fortunately the Last Adam, Jesus Christ, gave us the perfect example of what it means to submit to authority. Rather than using the word submission, Jesus said that we are to abide in His love, just like he abided in his father's love by obeying his commandments. Jesus loved God so much that he obeyed all the way to crucifixion on the cross.

---

1 Blue Letter Bible. "Dictionary and Word Search for hypotasso (Strong's 5293)". Blue Letter Bible. 1996-2013. 26 Jun 2013. < http:// www.blueletterbible.org/lang/lexicon/lexicon.cfm? Strongs=G5293&t=KJV >

As painful as it was to submit to God's authority during his torture and crucifixion, Jesus gave his life so that we could be reconciled and re-united to God as father. There is not greater love than this (John 15:13). Submission is about expressing love for God and for one another. It's all about a family and submitting to the head of the house. If we are in the family of God we must submit to him and his rules if we want to remain in the house. In God's House, the church, Jesus is the head, and when Jesus left the earth he said that he was sending us another comforter and guide who would lead us into all the truth. That comforter and guide is the Holy Spirit. Therefore every Christian that names the name of Jesus Christ should be operating as the spirit leads. Jesus said that if we love him, then we will obey him (John 14:21). If you love God, then submit to his authority and show him just how much you truly love him.

Like all the prophetic messages in this book, the words and explanations came directly from the Holy Spirit, in hopes of exhorting God's people to comply with his commands so that they might prosper in this earth.

Slaves Submit To Your Masters

Quite often when the first Apostles talked about love and submission, they would also include the relationships between slaves and their masters. In our modern day we could compare this to employees in a business or a household environment. It could also very well include the relationship that exists between church leaders and those under their leadership. In any case, the idea of submission is real. In fact, for the slaves during the days of the early church, it could have very well meant submission under extreme duress or even within a hostile environment. No matter the environment, the command remains the same.

Many times Christians will complain about the conditions at their place of employment. The number one complaint is, "I'm the only believer on the job." This seems hardly to be worthy of complaining because Jesus called us to be light in the midst of darkness. People in darkness do so not because they want to, many times it's out of habit or routine. Working hard is a mantra for many Americans. It goes back to the idea of sweating and toiling for a living, which was actually the curse God placed upon Adam (Genesis 3:17-19) for eating the forbidden fruit. One must remember that Jesus came to release us from that curse and to give us abundant live. That is why he said don't worry about what you should eat, or what you shall wear, but seek first the kingdom of God and his righteousness, and all these things will be added to you (Matthew 6:33). As believers, we no longer have to toil for a living. We make our living by submitting to the leadership of God through his Holy Spirit. If you are working at a place of employment, you should see yourself working for that employer as if your are working unto God. Also recognize that the Seedtime Harvest law is also in effect. That means that what ever you do for someone else, God will also make happen for you (Ephesians 6:8). So give that employer the best you've got!

Now in case you are working in a hostile environment, let me share a personal experience. The Lord has always sent me to employers where the staff was either in bondage or severely oppressed. Even one job was extremely hostile from the moment I walked in the door. After my first month on the job, a group of employees told me that they had been taking bets on whether I would make it past the first week. The staff was in turmoil and some crazy client was always threatening to either do bodily harm, or come shoot up the office with a gun. It was the job from hell, but I held down the fort for almost five years. God said that he sent me to break the curse off that business. I only remember complaining to the Lord only once about how I was disrespected. The Lord responded immediately, *"Now you know how I felt when they did it to me."* I quietly performed my job with excellence and the Lord told me that I was sowing seeds for a business that I would have one day. He promised that the manner in which I performed for that employer would one day be returned to me in my own company. That is how God expects us to submitted to an employer.

Sometimes, the most difficult place to work is in a ministry environment. I don't quite understand it, but when some believers are called by God and they know it, these "anointed" people can turn into prima donas. They can turn into monsters because now that they are anointed, they feel that there is no need for them to submit to any authority. The best advice in these cases is to submit to God in prayer and not let the prima dona lure you out of the spirit. If you are led by the spirit, you won't fall into your fleshly emotions. Also if you are under a strong spirit-led ministry, the leadership would have already identified the issue and they will take the initiative to bring the "anointed" one under control. If not, then this is your chance to intercede in prayer and God will prompt someone in the ministry to confront the issue.

Sometimes all it takes is for the leadership to remind them that every in the Body of Christ is anointed. That's why we are called Christians (the anointed ones). You beloved, stay in faith and remain in the place of blessing. Understanding and respecting God's kingdom hierarchy of command is the one of the priceless treasures worth obtaining. It is probably the most important as well. This is also the one area that throws believers into a tailspin out of control in misunderstanding. Just because you are called and anointed by God it doesn't mean that you no longer have to submit to authority. In fact, it means just the opposite. If God has a calling on your life, the only way you will successfully complete the call is if you submit not only to God, but to every man and woman God has placed in authority over you; whether that be at work, home or at church.

Finally, I want to address a sensitive employment situation that the Holy Spirit has brought to my attention: sexual harassment. Earlier this year, the Holy Spirit began guiding me into heavy intercession for some of America's most celebrated Black female artists and entertainers. In each case these women were in the midst of being physically and sexually brutalized by wealthy businessmen and industry executives. The women were trapped and were being made to fear for their lives. He says that America's obsession and insatiable appetite for pop stars and entertainment idols is feeding this predatory activity. According to the Lord, *"America's Idols Must Fall."* The Spirit of God says that no one is willing to blow the whistle on this industry accepted form of sex trafficking. I don't know exactly what the Lord is planning, but I do know he is about to take down oppressors in this and other industries and people will be set free.

If someone on your job is pressuring you with unwanted sexual advances, it is up to you to tell them to stop. If they refuse to listen, you may have to talk to a supervisor or manager with authority over the one harassing you. According to the U.S. Equal Employment Opportunity Commission (EEOC), 'Sexual harassment is a form of sex discrimination that violates Title VII of the Civil Rights Act of 1964. Title VII applies to employers with 15 or more employees, including state and local governments. It also applies to employment agencies and to labor organizations, as well as to the federal government. Unwelcome sexual advances, requests for sexual favors, and other verbal or physical conduct of a sexual nature constitute sexual harassment when this conduct explicitly or implicitly affects an individual's employment, unreasonably interferes with an individual's work performance, or creates an intimidating, hostile, or offensive work environment.'[1]

God hates oppression and abuse of any form. Cry out to him for help and he will answer you. His word promises that whosoever calls upon the name of the Lord shall be saved (Romans 10:13).

---

1 "Facts About Sexual Harassment." About EEOC/Publications. U.S. Equal Employment Opportunity Commission, n.d. Web. 27 June 2013. <http://www.eeoc.gov/facts/fs-sex.html>.

The Definition Of Marriage Is Submission

Submission in marriage is perhaps the most misunderstood and misused term. Many people are afraid of the word because so many men have used submission as a method of controlling and abusing their wives. Any man who thinks that God has given him Adam's authority to dominate and abuse his wife is dead wrong. This is a common excuse given by men who don't understand God's plan for the earth. Adam was never told to dominate Eve. He was told to dominate every animal that crept upon the earth. God created Eve as a helper, someone who would come along side of Adam to help him dominate the creatures of this earth (Genesis 1:26-28; 2:18-25).

In God's hierarchy, the woman submits to the man, who submits to Jesus, who submits to God. This rank was determined after the order of their appearance. God is supreme head overall. Then comes Jesus who is Lord over all men, and submitted to God. Man is head of the woman and submitted to Jesus. The headship of man was established when God created Adam. Since Adam was created first, he was put in charge. Eve came along later to help him do the work of God in the earth. The manner in which she was created (from his rib) lets you know that she was a part (subset of) Adam. A part of any thing can be equal to, but it can never be greater than the thing itself. That's a simple principle of elementary set theory, but it applies in this spiritual case as well. Jesus came from God; so he can never be greater than God; but in many ways he is equal to God; only not in rank. God is the established head.

So, in God's grand design there is no way that Eve, or women in general could ever outrank a man in marriage . . . however the lesser rank does come with its privileges. First and foremost, when all hell breaks loose, God will always hold the man responsible. Eve ate the forbidden fruit and gave it to Adam. They both ate it, but the sin was accounted to Adam because God commanded him directly (Genesis 3:17). It was his responsibility to see that God's will was done in that family, and God expects the same from men today.

Wives, don't even think about sabotaging your husbands just so God can put a hurting on them especially if you want your prayers answered. You are one flesh. If you sabotage him, you both will get hurt; and God will not hear your prayers (I Pet 3:7). Be courteous and compassionate towards one another; not rendering evil for evil so that you both can inherit the blessing. Wives, do not attempt to rule over your husband even if he is not walking in his full authority as head. Keep a quite and meek spirit while undergirding your spouse in prayer and God will bless you for it. Look at one another not just as husband and wife, but you are first and foremost members of the Body of Christ and brethren of the faith.

Even if you are married to a fool, God's got you covered. Remember Abigail (I Samuel 25)? She was the woman who was married to Nabal; a man whose name meant fool, and he definitely lived up to that name. He basically spit in the face of his soon-to-be king, David, after he and his men protected Nabal's flocks. David wanted to kill Nabal, and Abigail threw herself on the mercy of David. She was so loyal to this fool, that David blessed her in spite of her husband. Because both David and Abigail left things in God's hand, the Lord struck Nabal dead that next morning. When David heard that God defended him, he sent for Abigail and made her his wife. This is a perfect example of the power of submission. Rather than following their human instincts concerning Nabal, both Abigail and David submitted to God, and justice was done and no one had blood on their hands. God has a plan of operation that is more honorable and nobler than our human minds could ever imagine. Even if we don't agree, we must obey if we want God to bless us and honor us. Submission is beneficial in marriage, that's why both husband and wife are commanded to submit to one another in fear and reverence for God. What's good for one is even better for both when God and his blessings are the reward.

Key Scripture Reference

Ephesians 5:22-33
Wives, submit yourselves unto your own husbands, as unto the Lord. For the husband is the head of the wife, even as Christ is the head of the church: and he is the saviour of the body. Therefore as the church is subject unto Christ, so [let] the wives [be] to their own husbands in every

thing. Husbands, love your wives, even as Christ also loved the church, and gave himself for it; That he might sanctify and cleanse it with the washing of water by the word, That he might present it to himself a glorious church, not having spot, or wrinkle, or any such thing; but that it should be holy and without blemish.

So ought men to love their wives as their own bodies. He that loveth his wife loveth himself. For no man ever yet hated his own flesh; but nourisheth and cherisheth it, even as the Lord the church: For we are members of his body, of his flesh, and of his bones. For this cause shall a man leave his father and mother, and shall be joined unto his wife, and they two shall be one flesh.

This is a great mystery: but I speak concerning Christ and the church. Nevertheless let every one of you in particular so love his wife even as himself; and the wife [see] that she reverence [her] husband.

The Last Shall Be First And The First Shall Be Last

Some believe that the most segregated day in America is Sunday morning, as churches are divided up into various denominations and congregations that are separated by both doctrine and by race. Americans talk about tolerance for other races and cultures, but that is not what Jesus taught. He taught unconditional love. He told us to love our neighbor as we love ourselves. Few people actually hate themselves, and those that do, are locked inside a prison of personal horror. Most people like themselves, even too much. Narcissism is an issue in America. They place their needs above God and others. Both of these extremes are displeasing to God. Jesus says that we should do unto to others as we would have others do unto us (Luke 6:31). This is just the type of treatment we should have for others, not just in the church, but also along our daily paths of life. As we mentioned earlier, the Apostle Paul said that we should esteem other higher than ourselves.

There are church folk who can get along with those in their church, but disdain other believers. They render the same treatment even to the poor, the fatherless, the widow, the destitute and homeless. It goes back to that notion of Jesus being their personal savior and no more. There is nothing wrong with know that salvation is personal, but don't get this thing twisted. Jesus died for the entire world. He didn't die just for Christians, of just for your particular denomination or congregation. Jesus is a personal lord and savior for whosever would believe in him and follow his example.

The face of the church is beginning to not only to reflect our culture, but it also represents God's plan to make one family from every nation, tongue and tribe. Their song is being sung in heaven today, *"And they sung a new song, saying, Thou art worthy to take the book, and to open the seals thereof: for thou wast slain, and hast redeemed us to God by thy blood out of every kindred, and tongue, and people, and nation; And hast made us unto our God kings and priests: and we shall reign on the earth (Revelation 5:9-10). "* This was the plan of God since Adam. So even though a person may be a Muslim, Jew, Buddhists, or a non religious person today, once they hear the message of Jesus and the kingdom and believe what they hear, they will be translated into the Kingdom of God. As for those who continue to wreak havoc and want to do things their religious way, they may very well find themselves being thrown out of the kingdom as Jesus said. *"And whoso shall receive one such little child in my name receiveth me. But whoso shall offend one of these little ones which believe in me, it were better for him that a millstone were hanged about his neck, and that he were drowned in the depth of the sea* (Matthew 18:5-6). "

God is no respecter of persons, he is a rewarder of faith. In fact the Bible says that the eyes of the Lord run to and fro looking for someone, anyone whose heart is perfect toward him, so that he can show himself strong on their behalf. Again the Bible says that those who come to God must believe that he is, and that he is a rewarder of those who diligently seek him. It doesn't matter what you are or what you have been, God can turn it all around if you have faith enough to believe what he says. It's time for the church in America to repent for how they have treated the various people groups in our nation and in the world. Bigotry and racism are not allowed in God's kingdom. Jesus came to make all things equal with all men so that we might dwell with Father God as one big family both in heaven on earth. Families may disagree amongst each other, but in the end they always repent and come together for the greater good. That is what God is expecting, and don't be surprised if some of the most downtrodden souls are revived and thrust to the forefront of the faithful. God is about to reward them for believing him, even in dire circumstances. They may have given their all like the widow with the one mite, and in doing shall gain great esteem and kingdom treasure from their Father in heaven.

Key Scripture References

Matthew 19:27-30

Then answered Peter and said unto him, Behold, we have forsaken all, and followed thee; what shall we have therefore? And Jesus said unto them, Verily I say unto you, That ye which have followed me, in the regeneration when the Son of man shall sit in the throne of his glory, ye also shall sit upon twelve thrones, judging the twelve tribes of Israel. And every one that hath forsaken houses, or brethren, or sisters, or father, or mother, or wife, or children, or lands, for my name's sake, shall receive an hundredfold, and shall inherit everlasting life. But many [that are] first shall be last; and the last [shall be] first.

FEAR GOD

At first glance, the fear of the Lord appears quite ominous. It conjures up images of Almighty God sending wind and flood waters upon the earth like in Noah's day. It reminds us of the fire and brimstone raining down upon Sodom and Gomorrah as Abraham rescues Lot and his family from doom. It brings back memories of the plagues of Egypt and the River Nile turning to blood. Or even how the ground opened up and swallowed the rebels of Korah who dared to oppose the leader-ship of Moses. Even when the Children of Israel were in search of the Promised Land, God promised that the fear and dread of them would be upon the people because of the miraculous feats he performed against their enemies.

There is a myth in the American church that says God is a loving father who would never again do the things he did in the Old Testament. These people obviously never read the book of Revelation which tells how the kings of this earth gather for a final battle against God. It ends with Jesus riding in on his white horse with his chosen and faithful army and destroying the enemies of God with a great sword that comes out of his mouth. Too far fetched for your understanding? Let's bring it closer to home. Hebrews Chapter 12 puts things into perspective for the New Testament Christian. Chapter 11 talks about the faith and endurance of those under the old covenant. This is leads to a discussion to exhort believers to lay aside the weight and sin and run with patience (endurance) the race that our Lord has set before us. We are reminded of what it took for Jesus to endure the cross for us. Believers are exhorted to follow Jesus example, knowing that if they faint, the Lord would chasten them. Chastening is not pleasant for anyone, but it is necessary if we want to become obedient sons of God. The believer is then exhorted to correct that which is out of order with God; to walk in peace and holiness to insure that he or she would obtain their expected inheritance.

Perhaps the greatest argument for their obedience was given in Chapter 12:18-29, which describes what happened to those who wandered in the wilderness. They saw the Hand of God move mightily on their behalf. They saw the fire come down from heaven upon the mountain and it caused exceeding fear of God. That was the fear that came as a result of the old covenant. If God didn't spare the disobedient under the Moses' covenant, surely none would be spared under the new covenant that came from the blood sacrifice of God's son. If they did not escape punishment for refusing to obey the Lord as he spoke from the mountain, how can anyone escape from the one who speaks to us from heaven? His voice shook the earth back then, but God promises to shake both the heavens and the earth in our lifetime. The book of Hebrews ends with one final exhortation to stay obedient to the kingdom. The Kingdom of God is the one thing that will never be shaken. Therefore each believer should strive to be pleasing to God by serving him with reverence and godly fear; For our God is a consuming fire (Hebrews 12:28-29).

In short, if we honor and reverence Almighty God, we will have no trouble walking out our lives in the fear of him. His wrath is reserved only for the sons of disobedience; but for those who fear and honor God there is a promise of wealth, riches, honor and righteousness (Psalm 112). And, according to the Holy Spirit, God is about to "Raise a nation in the earth; a nation of those who are obedient to God. Power and glory shall be unto all who obey for it is the Glory of God Manifest in Men." This is the chosen generation, a royal priesthood, an holy nation, a peculiar people; that they would show forth the praises of him who has called them out of darkness into his marvellous light: Which in time past were not a nation, but are now they are the nation of God: which had not mercy, but now have obtained mercy.

Key Scripture References

Ecclesiastes 12:13-14
Let us hear the conclusion of the whole matter: Fear God, and keep his commandments: for this [is] the whole [duty] of man. For God shall bring every work into judgment, with every secret thing, whether [it be] good, or whether [it be] evil.

Worship the Creator Not The Creation

Although many people would love to believe that America is a Christian nation, it should be evident by our hot pursuit of the American Dream, that God really isn't at the center of our world, money is. The Lord calls America an *"Adulterous nation with many gods."* Most of what we do is for the love of money and the pride of life. We are so proud of what we have accomplished by our own efforts. Please don't misunderstand. There is nothing wrong with wanting accomplishments or wanting to have possessions; as long as we don't covet. Covetousness is a great sin against God because it places more value on the creation than it does the creator. This is idolatry. The same is true with money. Having money is not a sin; it's the love of money that drive humans to do every evil thing to get it (I Timothy 6:10). Again, there is nothing wrong with the American Dream until it causes pain, suffering and nightmares for ourselves and others. When men pursue things above God it always ends in loss and destruction. That is one of the reasons God reminded his people that it was he (God) who gave them the power to get wealth. He also promised that in the day that they forgot him and when they would begin saying that they got their wealth by their own hands, it would be into a curse to them (Deuteronomy 8:11-20). Unfortunately the same has happened in America. We haven't forgotten God, we just threw him out of our lives. This true in the church and the public sector.

For years the church has been receiving prophetic words about wealth being transferred to the people of God. Indeed, God is releasing great wealth and power within his kingdom; but not everyone who heard that word will reap the rewards of that word. Those who are obsessed with money will not be receiving from God (Mark 4:18-19). He will only reward those who love him and who will faithfully trust his word. You cannot serve both God and Mammon. We think that mammon is simply about money; but it is so much more. Mammon is a demon spirit who makes people a slave to money and riches. He makes people stoop to illegal or immoral means to get more; and leads them to kill or commit suicide when it's all gone. Mammon traps people with one convincing lie: there isn't enough to go around. He doesn't want us to trust God. Mammon wants men to destroy one another in the pursuit of wealth and riches.

Mammon will even make Christians rob God by withholding tithes and offerings (Malachi 3:8). Others will cheat their brothers and wonder why God won't bless them. Beloved, you lust after things you don't have, so you scheme and kill to get them. You are jealous of what others have, because you can't have it. You continue to fight and wage war to take things away from them. This is the spirit of Mammon. You don't have what you desire because you refuse to ask God for it (James 4:2). You refuse to do things God's way because you hate God and love Mammon.

God's riches are poured out upon those whom he loves. It's an unlimited supply that comes when we trust and obey God. Don't be distracted by the financial cares of this world. You may be desperate for money, but what you really need is wisdom. You need wisdom in making the right choices for your life, especially in touch financial times. Ask God. Seek His solution. Knock on heavens door to get your answer (Matthew 7:7). Any if any man lacks wisdom, on any subject, let him ask God (James 1:5). He will give you a solution that will produce supernatural results that can withstand the evil days. Trust God. He knows what you need. He just wants to be your only source so that you can be a partaker of the fullness of glory. Don't trust in uncertain riches. Have faith in God.

Key Scripture References

Matthew 6:24
No man can serve two masters: for either he will hate the one, and love the other; or else he will hold to the one, and despise the other. Ye can-not serve God and mammon.

Matthew 6:31-34
Therefore take no thought, saying, What shall we eat? or, What shall we drink? or, Wherewithal shall we be clothed? (For after all these things do the Gentiles seek:) for your heavenly Father knoweth that ye have need of all these things. But seek ye first the kingdom of God, and his righteousness; and all these things shall be added unto you. Take therefore no thought for the morrow: for the morrow shall take thought for the things of itself. Sufficient unto the day [is] the evil thereof.

Obey God For The Benefit Of All Men

I remember hearing a missionary on television describing the millions of children dying in Northeast Africa because there was no food. Normally I would hear these shows and be prompted to send a check, but this time it was different. In my heart I asked God, "When will this end? People have been talking about famine and poverty in Africa for generations. Why hasn't the famine lifted?" I knew that something was wrong. We see the same behavior in America. We keep throwing money into welfare programs to sustain people who still need to be sustained many years later. I knew in my heart that this was not God's plan. God gives us power to get wealth. He delights in the prosperity, not in the poverty of His People.

Then it hit my spirit! The Lord said he had given instructions to His People, but they refused to obey. There are many people in America who were given orders to travel and set up programs in some of the poorest nations of this world. Others were told to relocate to these impoverished areas but they did not move. *"American Christians have grown fat and comfortable in the USA,"* says God. They don't want to be inconvenienced by picking up and moving to areas where there may be no hotels, fast food, cable TV or Internet. God has blessed us with much, but it wasn't supposed to be wasted on our selfish desires. We were blessed to be a blessing. The Spirit of God says that there is no lack of resources, only a lack of obedient people who are willing to share their time and resources with others. This is the norm for American Christians. We refuse to *"Go into all the World"* as commanded by Jesus Christ, who we claim as our Lord and Savior.

Our command is an order for a peace keeping mission in another region of the world. It's a military position in the service of the Kingdom of God. Imagine what would happen if our US Military troops refused to obey their orders. The enemies of the world would run rampant. I thank God for the faithful men and women of our US military who are willing give up their lives so that we can live in peace and prosperity in America. But, didn't Jesus also tell his followers to give up their lives to serve him for the welfare of others? Yet so many American Christians only desire to serve themselves.

Our nation is faltering because as a people we have become selfish. The Lord said, *"We've become a nation of takers not givers."*[1] Many Americans have lost their compassion for the needy. Consequently, they have refused to obey the plan that God gave them for their families, communities and nation. All is not lost. God who is unwilling to let the cries of the people go unanswered, is sending out an army of obedient sons who are willing and ready to go boldly into devastated regions of the world using God's supernatural power to transform lives.

Here's something else to consider. Our obedience is not just about us. God knows how to maximize our obedience to the point that one person's obedience could cause many to be blessed. All we need do is to obey. The Lord said that miracles follow the path of an obedient believer. So while they are on the way to one place, miracles will break out all around them. He said that some of Jesus' greatest miracles happened as he was on his way somewhere else . . . and remember how people laid the sick in beds along the streets (Acts 5:15) so that Peter's shadow might heal them as he passed by? The same happens for every believer who will obey the command to *"Go."* God's glory emanates from the spirit of an obedient believer and changes the atmosphere around them. Healing, deliverance, provision and restoration happens along the path of every obedient believer. Just imagine what could happen if each of us actually worked together in obedience to God. We could change the world . . . and that is exactly God's plan for this earth. He's just waiting on us to obey. Beloved, Whatever he says do, do it!

Key Scripture References

Matthew 28:19-20
And Jesus came and spake unto them, saying, All power is given unto me in heaven and in earth. Go ye therefore, and teach all nations, baptizing them in the name of the Father, and of the Son, and of the Holy Ghost: Teaching them to observe all things whatsoever I have commanded you: and, lo, I am with you alway, [even] unto the end of the world. Amen.

John 2:5
Whatsoever he saith unto you, do [it].

---

1 Matthews, Paula. "God's Kingdom Economics/Seeking the Kingdom; Not a Job." American Heritage 101. Shaker Heights: Spirit & Life Publications[SM], 2012. 22. Print.

Return Your Hearts To God

God's greatest desire for America is that Christians would return their hearts back to him, but because we are a wealthy people, we count our success by our goods, and feel that we have need of nothing more. This is furthest from the truth. Our hearts are fat, and we don't understand that we are wretched and miserable, poor, blind and naked in the realm of the spirit (Revelation 3:17). People in our nation are suffering. Much prayer has gone forth, but there has been no answer. The Lord said, that *"your mouth is speaking, but your heart is far from him in fasting and prayer."* God will not hear nor respond to your selfish requires. In the company of your prayers, God hears the arguments and strivings you have with others. Your desire is to be right and to win an argument but your heart is not right with God. *"Do you want me to hear? Then humble your hearts before me. Instead of fasting and prayer to strive against another; do so for the benefit of another; to loose his bonds of spiritual captivity; to see the oppressed set free; feed the hungry, clothe the poor; give to him that has nothing then will I answer you. Stop your rebellion and heed my voice and I will heal your land of poverty, disease and financial lack. Obey me and I will return America her glory that I designed for her before the foundation of the world. I the Lord have spoken it and surely I will bring it to pass."*

Beloved, this is the word of God to his people, the church. If you want to be healed; if you want America to be healed, then we must stop doing our own thing and begin doing the God ordained thing for this hour. Repent. Follow the leading of the Holy Spirit. Seek the good of all men.

Key Scripture References

Isaiah 29:13-21 (The Message)
The Master said: "These people make a big show of saying the right thing, but their hearts aren't in it. Because they act like they're worshiping me but don't mean it, I'm going to step in and shock them awake, astonish them, stand them on their ears. The wise ones who had it all figured out will be exposed as fools. The smart people who thought they knew everything will turn out to know nothing."

Doom to you! You pretend to have the inside track. You shut God out and work behind the scenes, Plotting the future as if you knew every-thing, acting mysterious, never showing your hand. You have every-thing backward! You treat the potter as a lump of clay. Does a book say to its author,"He didn't write a word of me"? Does a meal say to the woman who cooked it,"She had nothing to do with this"?

And then before you know it, and without you having anything to do with it,Wasted Lebanon will be transformed into lush gardens, and Mount Carmel reforested. At that time the deaf will hear word-for-word what's been written. After a lifetime in the dark, the blind will see. The cast-offs of society will be laughing and dancing in God, the down-and-outs shouting praise to The Holy of Israel.

For there'll be no more gangs on the street. Cynical scoffers will be an extinct species. Those who never missed a chance to hurt or demean will never be heard of again: Gone the people who corrupted the courts, gone the people who cheated the poor, gone the people who victimized the innocent.

Isaiah 58:13-14 (KJV)
If thou turn away thy foot from the sabbath, [from] doing thy pleasure on my holy day; and call the sabbath a delight, the holy of the LORD, honourable; and shalt honour him, not doing thine own ways, nor finding thine own pleasure, nor speaking [thine own]words: Then shalt thou delight thyself in the LORD; and I will cause thee to ride upon the high places of the earth, and feed thee with the heritage of Jacob thy father: for the mouth of the LORD hath spoken [it].

II Chronicles 7:14 (KJV)
If my people, which are called by my name, shall humble themselves, and pray, and seek my face, and turn from their wicked ways; then will I hear from heaven, and will forgive their sin, and will heal their land.

HONOR THE KING

The heart of the king is in the hand of the Lord, and like rivers of water, the Lord guides him as he wishes. That's what Proverbs 21:1 says, and yet few Christians actually believe that this is true. How do I know? Observe their actions and comments concerning those who have been elected as President in America. It doesn't matter who is in office. Christian leaders will have something negative to say about how things are being run in the White House, and unfortunately this serves as an ugly example for the church. God's word is very clear in explaining how his people should render honor to those whom honor is due. It is a constant theme throughout the Bible, but God's people apparently are not getting the message.

Romans 13:1-4 commands us to submit to the higher powers in civil government. It doesn't say to submit only if you agree with the policies of that power. It doesn't say to submit if you approve of who is in power; it simply commands us to submit. When we submit to the civil powers it gives honor to the office the person holds, and it gives honor to God; for there is no power except from God; and the powers that be, are ordained of God. Jesus gave us the perfect example of submitting to the higher powers. He never tried to overthrow the ruler of any nation, other than satan, the prince of the Kingdom of Darkness. Pilate tried to exert political pressure on Jesus by reminding him that he (Pilate) had authority to have him killed or released. Jesus responded by letting Pilate know that he would have no power against him at all if God had not given it to him. Jesus submitted to Pilate's authority as unto God and was put to death (John 19:10-11). The passage in Romans continues by saying that those who resist the power resists what God has ordained, and whoever resists shall bring upon himself damnation. King Saul was such an example. He lost his throne because he stepped out of his authority to perform duties that were to be done by the prophet Samuel. When God took his spirit away from Saul and anointed David to be king, Saul tried to kill David and it ended up costing him life and that of his sons. On the other hand, David honored Saul, even as his life was threatened. God honored David greatly because he knew what it mean to touch not my anointed and do my prophets no harm (I Chronicles 16:22). Any power ordained by God is also appointed and anointed by him. If God ordained the power then that power is a minister of God for good and is only a terror to those who do evil. This same rule of honor applies to the powers in the church. We are even called to give double honor to those elders who rule well, especially those who preach and teach the word of God (I Timothy 5:17).

When we honor the powers in authority over us, we do so knowing that our faith is in God and not in that authority alone. If God ordained the power, then God alone can moved the heart of any authority for the good of his people. Jesus tells a parable about an unjust judge who does not fear God and he doesn't care for people (Luke 18:1-8). There was a widow who came to the judge and asked him to avenge her of her adversary and the judge would not. This widow kept coming back to the judge and he kept refusing her until one day he said that although he didn't fear God and didn't care about people, he knew he had to do something to keep this widow from worrying him. The Lord said, *Hear what the unjust judge saith. And shall not God avenge his own elect, which cry day and night unto him, though he bear long with them? I tell you that he will avenge them speedily. Nevertheless when the Son of man cometh, shall he find faith on the earth* (Luke 18:8)?" There you have it! Honoring those in authority has to do with faith. Do we believe that God will do what his word says he will do through the powers that he has ordained, whether avenging an enemy or receiving justice in this world. If we pray without ceasing and work righteousness, that allows God's authority to move upon all the authorities of this earth. The prophet Isaiah prophesied that if God's people would cease from doing evil and learn how to do good by seeking God's justice, rebuking the oppressor, defending the widow and the fatherless, then the Lord would make sure that our judges and counselors (advisors and attorneys) work righteousness on our behalf (Isaiah 1:1-27).

In short, when we do our part, God is able to do his part in implementing justice. Proverbs 16:7 says that when a man's ways please God that even his enemies will be at peace with him. So, if we don't believe God, then we have no faith; and without faith it is impossible to please him (Hebrews 11:6). Honor requires that we have confidence in God and not in human abilities alone. We pray in confidence and obey God in confidence knowing that whatever we ask, we shall receive because we do our part in keeping his commandments and by doing what is right in God's eyes (I John 3:20). One of the main reasons Christians in America have not seen a righteous outcome in our nation is because those who are praying have unclean hearts and dirty hands. They speak words of division and strife with the intent of doing evil. Do not render evil for evil. If you hold iniquity in your heart, God will not hear your prayer (Psalm 66:18). God will work miraculously in your situation. Let the Holy Spirit guide you into the truth, that is his job. There is a spiritual principle in operation where things are being done by *the finger of God; by the word and power of God*. The Lord told me that whenever a believer obeys the instructions of the Holy Spirit in a specific situation, it causes the laws of God's kingdom to supercede every law in this universe. That includes all physical and governmental laws. To explain how this principle works, the Lord took me to Luke 11:14-20 when Jesus was casting out a devil and he was accused of casting out devils by Beelzebub the chief of the devils. Jesus said that if he cast out devils by the finger of God, then the kingdom of God had come upon them. The kingdom of God is both a place and a method of operating in this earth, that even causes supernatural favor to move in your direction as God moves upon the hearts of those in authority. Honoring those in authority means honoring God's way of operating which results in supernatural manifestations of God's word.

American Christians often curse themselves by abandoning God's word to rely on the arm of the flesh, and on *the system* to get what they want in this world (Jeremiah 17:5). If you are having issues obeying authority, ask the Holy Spirit to instruct you. He need only send the word and God's supernatural power would intervene. Remember the centurion with the servant that was sick (Matthew 8:5-13)? He came to Jesus saying that his servant was sick with the palsy and he was grievously ill. Jesus offer to go to centurion's home to heal the servant, but the centurion say that he felt unworthy of having Jesus come to his home. Instead he told Jesus to *speak the word only* and his servant would be healed, *For I am a man under authority, having soldiers under me: and I say to this [man], Go, and he goeth; and to another, Come, and he cometh; and to my servant, Do this, and he doeth [it]*. After hearing this Jesus marvelled and said, *Verily I say unto you, I have not found so great faith, no, not in Israel.* Here was an army officer who not only recognized the authority of God's kingdom in the ministry of Jesus, but he also understood the ability of word to carry out the desires of that authority. *And Jesus said unto the centurion, Go thy way; and as thou hast believed, [so] be it done unto thee. And his servant was healed in the selfsame hour.*

God has called us to honor those in authority over our lives so that the kingdom can be manifested in our world, and we can prosper in the land. The word works, if only we would believe. There is no need for us to rebuke our elders or speak evil of our political leaders. To do so is to speak evil of that which God has ordained. We don't even have to jockey for a position to be heard. If God wants you to speak, let the Holy Spirit give you the words so that you speak as the oracles of God. Obey God and honor his chosen authority. No matter how evil you perceive that authority to be, stay in faith. Nothing is impossible with God when we believe. Have faith in God.

Submit to the ruling authorities, not only to avoid the wrath of God, but also for conscience sake. This is also why we are also commanded to pay taxes and tribute. These are ministers of God. Therefore render to them what they are due: tribute to whom tribute is due; custom to whom custom; fear to whom fear; honor to whom honor.

We will continue in his section to show how honor should be displayed in our civic duties and how to recognized God's covenant operating in the leadership he has chosen.

Honoring Civic Duties

The Spirit of God impressed upon me that believer's in America are sorely lacking in their civic responsibility. We've abandoned the ideals of both our country and our God for our own selfish desires. We longer love God above all people, things and desires. We no longer love our neighbor more than ourselves. This is not the spirit nor the character of our Lord, and it definitely is not beneficial to our nation.

We are commanded to submit to every ordinance of man for the Lord's sake, in order to silence the ignorance of foolish men who don't believe what we believe. We are to live as free men, not using our liberty as a cloak for concealing evil, but as good citizens and servants of God (I Peter 2:13-16).

The U.S. Department of Homeland Security[1] identifies several key responsibilities of American citizens. God expects believers to honor them all, including defending and supporting the Constitution, voting, respecting the rights and beliefs of others, serving on a jury when called, paying taxes and respecting and obeying the laws of this nation. Here is a prime example. There has been much debate about gay marriage. On June 26, 2013, The Supreme Court has ruled against at least a portion of the Defense of Marriage Act (DOMA),[2] that legally defined marriage in the United States. In May of 2012, the Holy Spirit shared the Lord's view on gay marriage. He said, ***"Gays are looking for love any way they can find it. Love is what ever person desires. But now legal remedies are being sought in order to protect gays from the hatred of men. This ought not be because it should have never elevated to this point."*** Unfortunately, many Christians will find it hard to believe that the Lord saw this one coming. The Lord said that if it had not been for the Christians who used their political voice to attack the gays, the legalities may not have occurred.

---

1 "Responsibilities of a Citizen." The Citizen's Almanac: Fundamental Documents, Symbols, and Anthems of the United States. [Washing-ton, D.C.]: U.S. Citizenship and Immigration Services, U.S. Dept. of Homeland Security, Office of Citizenship, 2010.5-8.Print.
2 "United States v Windsor." Supremecourt.gov. The Supreme Court of The United States, 26 June 2013. Web. 30 June 2013. <http://www. supremecourt.gov/opinions/12pdf/12-307_6j37.pdf>.

In America there are many people groups and many religious beliefs. Christians are to be the light to the nation by demonstrating their faith with love and compassion for others; but we cannot, under any circumstance violate the rights of citizens who do not act or think like we do. God commands us to honor every ordinance whether we believe in it or not; and yes there will be challenges at times where the law of the land may violate our core beliefs, but it need not hinder our faith in God's ability to intervene on our behalf when we obey him. Pray for those who are in authority over the various branches of our government. Pray that the will of God will be done for the sake of all men so we can lead a quiet and peaceable life in all godliness and honesty (I Timothy 2:1-2).

Also exercise your right to vote. Every believer should be fasting and praying about the issues and the candidates, before each election, realizing that God is neither a republican nor is he a democrat. He is no respecter of persons. He looks at their hearts. God can choose whom he pleases and influence their politics. While the voting record shows some tendencies of a candidate, it does not tell the whole story. God alone knows who is to lead his people. Ask God how you should vote and then vote accordingly. It doesn't matter if the person is a believer or not. If God said vote for that person, then obey God. Don't try to figure it out. God's thoughts and his ways are higher than ours, but if we obey him, the word will accomplish the thing that God desires (Isaiah 55:8-11).

There are some Christian leaders who tell their congregations to vote to let the politicians know how they feel. Need I remind you that we walk by faith and not by sight or by how we feel? Whenever a Christian carries out any decision because of an emotion, such as anger, they have made a "fleshly" decision, which according to Galatians 6:8 will only bring destruction. We are commanded to sow (carry out decisions) in the Spirit. That means to pray and seek God for direction, then obey what he tells you. If every Christian in America would just obey God, our nation would flourish. There is an evangelistic reason for obeying God at the ballot box. The Gospel of Jesus Christ is about changing the hearts and behavior of men on earth. There could be someone who has a heart to help the people and he or she doesn't yet know God. This is exactly the kind of person God could use to create a miraculous move in the right direction.

Remember Jesus' disciples? They were unlearned and ignorant to the ways of religion, yet God used them to transform the world (Acts 4:13). If we as Christians pray for those in authority as we are commanded, then we can cause the power of God to rule in every decision that politician makes, and in the process transform a soul for the Kingdom, and transform our nation!

Beloved, vote not according to your political party or your own ideas, vote as the Holy Spirit leads you to vote, and you will be sowing seeds of righteousness that will open up kingdom benefits for ourselves, our families and our nation. It's like Jesus said, when we obey (God) or act with *the finger of God*, then the Kingdom of God will come upon us and shower us with all heaven has to offer.

"In this season one can only gain prosperity if they are following and honoring one who is in covenant with me. It is a supernatural blessing of immense proportions for all who would believe and receive," says God. The Lord always honors those who honors his covenant. God made a covenant with his son Jesus, a covenant that was sealed with Jesus' blood. Many people argue that Israel is the only nation that has a covenant with God. This is not true. When the Puritans came to our shores, they did so to honor God. They solidified their honor by making a covenant with Almighty God in the Mayflower Compact of 1620. Once a covenant is made with God, it can never be broken, and herein lies a true blessing. Although America's chance to become a Christian nation is a missed opportunity," the Lord said that we do have one "ace in the hole." Not only did the Puritan covenant with God, so did many other people throughout American history. There is also, a remnant of believers who still hold dear to that covenant, and God is about to make good on every promise he has made to every generation. It's not only for the benefit of the believer. A covenant with the Almighty ensures that whenever America or her people are in trouble, if we would only turn our hearts and minds to God (regardless of our religious beliefs), he will remember the covenant, hear our prayers and heal our land.

Key Scripture References

Deuteronomy 7:9
Know therefore that the LORD thy God, he [is] God, the faithful God, which keepeth covenant and mercy with them that love him and keep his commandments to a thousand generations.

Ruth 1:16-17
And Ruth said, Intreat me not to leave thee, [or] to return from following after thee: for whither thou goest, I will go; and where thou lodgest, I will lodge: thy people [shall be] my people, and thy God my God: Where thou diest, will I die, and there will I be buried: the LORD do so to me, and more also, [if ought] but death part thee and me.

The follow prophecy was published on November 3, 2012. It tells of the Hand of God that is upon our president and our nation. It's a strong word. It's a humbling word for all the naysayers, because it also tells of God's everlasting love for America. It is a word that should revive the fear of the Lord in the heart of every true believer.

"The 2012 Election is not about Democrats, Republicans, or about the economy, abortion, gay rights or taxes. "No! No! No" says God. "It's about the prosperity of America. Yeah, Have I not said that 2012 is the Year of Increase? My word has not changed. The prosperity awaits you, but you must obey to receive. Any man who speaks evil of the American economy or about job losses is a false prophet. This is not my plan. This is the voice of demonic oppression that wants to enslave the American people. I have said it and will continue to say that Increase awaits you America, but the choice is yours. My servant Obama has prosperity in his hands; an anointing I have given him to prosper the nations of the world. He has the plan; it is a supernatural plan that I have designed first for America, and then for the rest of the world. It is done says God. I love America too much to let her fail. She came after me. She sought me out at the foundation of this nation. Such a demonstration of love has never been proven by any nation, not even Israel whom I sought after . . . No, it is and always has been America because she came to me with a willing heart to create a Promised Land flowing with milk and honey; a prosperous land that will undergird the nations of the world."

This is my plan. It will be done by Mr. Obama and the remnant I have chosen to bring this nation; my beloved child America back to her place of greatness in me. And oh, how the nations who have counted her out, will turn and see my magnificence upon her and they will run to her shores to learn about me and my Kingdom that will operate on this earth as it is in heaven. How is it in heaven you ask? It's my glorious home where there is only wealth, healing and unlimited supply of every good thing, and it is yours for the asking America. Obama has the plan. He is the man that I have chosen for this task in this hour; for such a time as this."

"The opposition will be sadden and will seek to retaliate against the man I have chosen, but know this, to retaliate against him will be a retaliation against me" says, God. "They are men of great wealth and power who have illegal and immoral ways of oppressing the poor. This demonic is embedded in their institutions. They claim to be people of faith, but they know not me, or my ways. They are impostors who lead astray simple minds who are impressed by their much learning and gathering of wealth. They are hoarders whom I have cursed in this season. If they change not their ways, they will lose their wealth. If they continue to fight against me, they will lose their lives. I am God and will not be mocked by any man; no matter how much wisdom and wealth he has gained. It all belongs to me, and I decide who has possession of the wealth. You evil rich men have brought this country to the ruin, but I have a people amongst you who have been given the plan to prosper America. I will take your wealth and give it to them. They have my heart for the people. They have my anointing to get my plan done in the earth. This my Kingdom hour to demonstrate my goodness and mercy to all mankind, and it will be done in America whom I have chosen for this demonstration so that all men can see that I am God and I have always loved my human creation; and have only plans to do you good and not evil. I love you, come to me and see the great and mighty plan I have for your lives."

Key Scripture Reference

Zechariah 8:20-23

Thus saith the LORD of hosts; [It shall] yet [come to pass], that there shall come people, and the inhabitants of many cities: And the inhabitants of one [city] shall go to another, saying, Let us go speedily to pray before the LORD, and to seek the LORD of hosts: I will go also. Yea, many people and strong nations shall come to seek the LORD of hosts in Jerusalem, and to pray before the LORD. Thus saith the LORD of hosts; In those days [it shall come to pass], that ten men shall take hold out of all languages of the nations, even shall take hold of the skirt of him that is a Jew, saying, We will go with you: for we have heard [that] God [is] with you.

CONCLUSION
How To Please God And Change The World

In America we talk about Jesus being our *"personal savior."* Many people take this to mean that *"it's all about me. Jesus came only for me."* Although the Bible does not refer to Jesus as a personal savior per se, I do believe that the original intent was for individuals coming to Christ to recognize their importance to God, but somewhere we got it twisted and think that we alone are important to God. There are pastors and leaders in the church who brag about being "anointed" as if it is a special status among believers. Truth is, anyone who names Jesus as Lord is anointed because the Holy Spirit resides within them. This attitude stems from the notion that God only chooses one person among the Body of Christ to use mightily. I've heard people talk about someone or other being "God's Man." Which implies that they were separated and anointed for greatness above other believers. This is also not true. God has a plan and purpose for every life that comes into his kingdom, but he cannot give a greater anointing for service unless we yield ourselves for his use. God is no respecter of persons, he rewards us according to our faith. The Bible says that God is able to do exceedingly abundantly more than we could ask or think according to the power that works in us. If we have faith enough to believe what God wants to do with our lives, then we will obey him and give the Holy Spirit license to use our gifts and talents to change the world.

In my case, the Holy Spirit didn't say anything to me about God's plan for my life until I went through a tragic divorce. I asked why so many evil things were happening to me and the Lord replied that is wasn't so much about what I had done, but what He had planned for me to do in this earth. This was the first time I had knowledge of the fact that God had a specific plan for my life. I remember asking him, "How was I supposed to know this? No one ever told me you had a plan for my life."I was saved at a early age in life, but the idea of service to God outside of my local church, never occurred to me. It wasn't until the I received the gift of the Holy Spirit, that the Lord began revealing the specifics of his call on my life. I always thought I knew what I wanted for my life, but the Lord told me, ***"You know nothing about your life!"*** These words shocked me.

Of course I knew what I wanted, or at least I thought I did. Like many of those in pursuit of the American Dream, I had gone to college, entered the work force in the area of my choice and was enjoying a great deal of success. I experienced financial freedom enough to do and buy whatever I wanted. I even had a thirty-year plan for my life. Why shouldn't I know what I wanted? Then the Lord said words that turned my life around and set me on the right track. He said **unless I consulted with him, I knew nothing about my life. He said that he didn't save me so that I could work my plan. Being saved meant surrendering my life to his plan.** In that one conversation, I learned that my gifts and talents were given to me to be used for God's purpose, not mine.

Jesus died so that we which live should not henceforth live unto ourselves, but unto him which died for us, and rose again (II Corinthians 5:15). We were bought with a price: therefore we are commanded to glorify God in our bodies, and in our spirits, which are God's (II Corinthians 6:20). This was a major revelation that drastically changed my life. There was some good news about the choices I had made in my life to that point. The Holy Spirit let me know that he was directing my steps to a degree, but the mystery of his plan for my life would not begin to unfold until I moved into greater depths of his spirit. Greater depths in God meant a greater surrender on my part. I had to decrease so that God could increase in my life.

The first step toward my process of surrender was to receive the power of the Holy Spirit. The Lord took me through the Bible and began showing me that since the fall of Adam, he had been looking for someone who would obey him in order to receive the inheritance that Adam lost. He also told me that I needed his power in order to possess all he had for me. The Lord commanded me to go to Los Angeles on a quest to find his power. I felt much like Abraham when he left Ur of the Chaldees. The Lord just said go. When I asked where I would live or how I would support myself, he told me to seek first his kingdom and those things would be provided for me. So, with fifty dollars cash and a credit card in my wallet I left my family and drove over 2,000 miles to Los Angeles. This left many wondering if my trip to LA was my big break in Hollywood, it was my big break, but not in the way people thought it would be.

Once again, I am reminded of when Jesus resurrected and met with his disciples, they asked him if he was going to restore again the kingdom on this earth at that time. The kingdom would be restored, but not in the way they had thought. This was the same thing the Lord was telling me. People were looking for me to do something big and I was also looking at God to do something big in my life. He said that everything I had lost would be restored to me in Los Angeles. The Lord also said that all of my dreams would be fulfilled by going to Los Angeles. I had no particular dreams in mind at that time, but soon there came an outpouring of God's dreams and promises. More than I could ever imagine. I delighted myself in the Lord and he put his desires in my heart (Psalm 37:4).

I got a crash course in God's way of doing things. I quickly learned that the Kingdom of God is more than just a place, it is a method of operating in the earth using spiritual principles set in place by God. It begins inside the heart of every believer. So rather than looking for some big event to break through the skies, every believer should be looking within their hearts and listening to every word the Holy Spirit is speaking to their spirits. In our day, the church is looking for heaven to take them out of here so they can see the kingdom of God. The goal is not to go to heaven, but to bring heaven down to earth; and it all begins with each individual believer walk king by faith in the thing that God has called him or her to do.

Christians are always looking for Jesus to step out of heaven to do some-thing on earth. Truth is, he already did that. Remember when he said *"It is finished,"* the Lord was talking about his assignment on the earth. It was finished at the cross. When he resurrected with all the power in heaven and earth, he commanded his disciples to take hold of that power and go into the earth doing what he did. Our assignment is to take the benefits of the cross and all the power it granted us and complete our part in bringing the kingdom to earth. It's not about church. It's not about obtaining a position in the church. We, the people of God are the church, the elect, the ones called out from our place in this world to fulfill our positions in the kingdom, a position that only the Holy Spirit can reveal to you. Eyes have not seen, nor have ears heard, neither has it entered into the hearts of men what God has planned for those who will love and obey him. It is revealed by the spirit. So you have to be attuned to the Holy Spirit in order to know your true call and assignment in this earth.

We are the Body of Christ, elected and appointed to operate in all the power of heaven and earth in Jesus' stead. Each member of the Body has a specific function to perform. When we begin operating in our authority and under submission to heaven, the earth will see no difference between Jesus and those acting in his name.

We would then be in unity with God the father, Jesus the son and with the Holy Spirit as one heart and one soul in one accord with the plan and purpose of heaven. It all begins with every member of the Body determining to surrender their lives and let the Spirit be lord once and for all. Most Christians have yet to grasp this mystery of the kingdom because they are too busy in church programs and political agendas to be able to stop and listen to what the spirit is speaking. Yet, they are looking for Jesus to come back to rule, when he is still waiting for his Body to take the abundance of grace and the gift of righteous and actually rule and reign in this life. He told us to *"Occupy"* till he comes back. Therefore, the restoration of the kingdom on earth begins with each of us manifesting the kingdom agenda placed within our hearts, and becoming sons of God manifesting the glory of God on earth. This is the kingdom of God manifested on men. Again, the disciples were looking for Jesus to return and reign upon the earth and the Lord told them to receive power from the Holy Spirit, but he told them to do so for a specific purpose. So that they would become witnesses to him in Jerusalem, and in Judea, and Samaria and to the uttermost parts of the world. How does that translate in the church today? When we obey the Holy Spirit it produces questions about the kingdom in the minds of unbelievers. Any time Jesus or the Apostles performed miraculous works it caused a stir among common observers. Then followed questions about how this thing happened. What power caused this thing to happen? Who are you and who gave you this authority? As God's servants answered these questions, they were giving witness of the kingdom of God. Sometimes the criticism was negative and persecution broke loose. Other times people immediately believed in the resurrection power of God and they received Jesus as Lord and Savior. Whether observers believed or not, everyone saw and experienced something that was unusual and supernatural. This is how Jesus intended for the world to know that the kingdom was at hand. This is what it means to be a witness of the kingdom, but it can only be done by those who have received the Holy Spirit and who will obey and do whatever he tells them to do.

Notice that Jesus does not have to have an earthly throne or physical territory in order for God's kingdom to reign. God's kingdom can reign in the midst of darkness because the light of his kingdom resides in the hearts of his faithful believers. The prophet Isaiah spoke about a time when darkness would cover the earth and gross darkness the people, but the glory of God would be seen upon his people. It would arise like a beacon light in the darkness; so bright that people would be drawn to it to find refuge and safety (Isaiah 60:1-3). The strength of the kingdom is that it's power causes God's people to rule in the midst of their enemies (Psalm 110:2). There is something about the darkness that causes the glory of God to shine ever so bright. So, if you are expecting a pretty transition from the kingdom of darkness to that of God's kingdom rule, forget it. God send his people into utter darkness to beat the enemy on his own territory. Psalm 16 describes the time after Jesus died and descended into hell. God promised not to leave his soul in hell and that his body would not see corruption. Jesus ascended from hell and now sits at the right hand of God. He declared that he is the one that was dead and now lives forevermore. It is he that possesses both the keys to hell and death (Revelation 1:18). How did he do all of that? Jesus came to earth so that he could take the power of death out of the hands of Satan. The Apostle Paul said that Jesus spoiled principalities and the evil powers and made an open show of them by what he did on the cross (Colossians 2:15). The enemy has always used death and the fear of death to rule over men on earth. Jesus proved that the power of the kingdom could defeat death once and for all. That is why he had to die, go to hell and resurrection. This was the ultimate witness of the power of God's kingdom.

Many Christians who feel powerless again Satan and his demonic forces in this earth are those who have no idea that they have been given authority over all of the power of the enemy. That it is why it is important for us to follow the Holy Spirit. The plan of God for our lives will always include miraculous feats that will make an open show of the devil, and it's especially insulting when we defy death on enemy territory and come out victorious. Not only do we come out, but we also set the captives free. This is how the power of the kingdom will manifest upon men in every area of life on earth. Believers have to actually believe what God says above all other voices. The Lord wants to demonstrate his power through us. He wants to do exceeding abundantly above all that we could ask or think, but it is strictly according to the power we allow to work through us. No power; no miracles. No miracles, no witness. No witness, no glory upon our lives. God wants his glory seen upon us in these times of gross darkness. If we allow the Holy Spirit to lead us, we will always come out victorious. The Lord will prepare a table before us in the presence of our enemies. He will anoint our heads with oil, and fill our cups until it overflows. Imagine the boldness of God to send his people into utter darkness and pour out his spirit and resources so much that those in darkness would be transformed by the light of his kingdom . . . and God's kingdom will destroy all other kingdoms. God's kingdom will remain forever. So, whatever we bring forth out of our spirits in obedience, it will also remain forever. This is how we begin to take back territory for the kingdom. Each of us has to do our part.

Now that we know what it means to be a witness for God's kingdom, what did Jesus mean when he told the disciples that they would witness for him in Jerusalem, and Judea and Samaria and the uttermost parts of the earth? Does each believer have to go to these specific places in order to be obedient? Not necessarily. It depends on where you received your commission to be a witness. When the first Apostles got their commissions, they were already in Jerusalem awaiting the Holy Spirit. Therefore Jesus wanted them to begin witnessing for him right where they were. From Jerusalem they began spreading out into the outlying regions until eventually they moved into all of the world.

Where and how the Apostles moved also depended upon how they were received in a particular location. You may remember that although the Lord poured out his spirit and there were great miracles. There was also great persecution that drove the many witnesses out of Jerusalem and into the other regions. Jesus had trained his disciples to go where they were received. If town or house rejected them and their message, they were told to shake the dust off of the shoes and move on to the next city. That is pretty much the way it is today. Everyone God calls has a Jerusalem. It's the place where they met God and received their commission to go be a witness. Some people are able to stay in their Jerusalem for a long while before persecution forces them out of a city; but if they prove faithful regardless of the persecution, they will be greatly rewarded.

My Jerusalem was Hollywood, California. Since I was working in the television and film industry when God called me, it was natural for Hollywood to be my mission field. In addition, the Lord said that he was sending me out like he did the first Apostles. The Lord sent me to pastors, leaders and churches in many cities. My job was to help them get back on track with God's assignment. Most were under severe demonic attack. My assignment was to provide much needed outside spiritual muscle to defeat the enemy and help the leaders to repair the breach in their ministries. As I proved myself faithful, the Lord began sending me around the nation. When I performed faithfully in the nation, he began sending me to other countries. Since then, the Lord has given me a global plan for my assignment. This was also one of the reason, I never got the big break people were expecting. It's all in God's timing.

The Lord wanted me to see my purpose from the kingdom point of view, first. He wanted me to seek first the kingdom. In the world, we seek money and fame first, and foremost. God is planning a global takeover. His plan for my life was much bigger than fame and fortune. God was giving me instructions for projects and ideas that would transform lives around the world. While I was looking at a thirty-year plan for my life, the Lord gave me a fifty-year plan for corporations he wanted me to build. He told me that this was just the beginning of what he wanted me to do. It's not church as usual because those whom God is calling in this hour will step forward in all the power and glory of the kingdom. The Lord will prove to the church and to the world, that his thoughts are not like our thoughts neither are his ways like ours. His plans for our lives are bigger than anything we could ever imagine on our own (Ephesians 3:20).

The commission Jesus gave the first Apostles is still relevant today, and it will prove to me more dynamic than ever. The Lord calls them the *"Last Apostles."* Imagine an army of believers doing greater exploits than the prophets of old, Jesus Christ and all the Apostles combined. These are the greater works that Jesus said would be done in the earth. Those whom God will be using are those who have sold out to the kingdom. The Lord said that they will obey God no matter the circumstance. These are those who will imitate God the father and walk in the ways of Jesus.

When Jesus was baptized it was the Glory of God that spoke from Heaven and declared, *"This is my beloved Son, in whom I am well pleased."* Jesus had not started his earthly ministry and yet God was well pleased. How could this be? Jesus came into the earth for one purpose and one purpose only: to do the will of God (Hebrews 10:7; Psalm 40:7-8). Jesus came with a heart that was wholly submitted to the will of God. There is a season of God's Glory approaching and the Lord wants you to be prepared. The Glory is the physical manifestation of God's word in the earth. This means whatever words God has spoken will come to pass for those who are speaking and obeying those same words. It all begins and ends with Jesus; the one who poured out his life showing us how to manifest the goodness of God's Glory in the earth. Jesus didn't do his own thing on earth; he only did what God told him. He only spoke the words that the Holy Spirit gave him to speak. Jesus was a true imitator of God in the earth. And guess what? Jesus knew that someday we would be just like him; walking and talking like God and manifesting the glory in the earth. In John 12:28 Jesus said, *Father, Glorify thy name; and there came a voice from heaven saying, 'I have both glorified and will glorify again.* Jesus and the Father were referring to us; the modern-day obedient believers. Jesus even said that we would do greater works than he did in the earth (John 14:12).

Some people believe that the greater works will be performed because there will be more people operating in the power of God since Jesus walked the earth. This is true; but there will also be works of greater magnitude than we have seen on the earth because as we approach Jesus' return to earth there will be greater darkness for us to overcome with our faith. As we said earlier in this book, every prophecy that has not come to pass, must do so in this season of glory. Of course there are prophecies dealing with Jesus' return, the passing away of the current heavens and earth, and the New Jerusalem. Others will come to pass in the next millennium and beyond. For those of us on the earth in the hour when the church is ushering in the kingdom, those prophecies about the earth and it's inhabitants must come to pass in this season of God's glory. So, the greater works we will see will have to do with the end-time harvest of souls into the kingdom. There are also strategic programs and developments that God has ordained for business, governments and industries around the world that will also begin to operate in kingdom mode.

Little is said in the Bible about the specific things God has for the church to do before his return. Many speculate on which nations will even be in existence when Jesus comes back, because the Bible spends much time prophesying about Israel, but this prophet knows for sure that whatever God has planned for the nations, America is in the forefront. As our prophecies stated in this book, God has a special place in his heart for America because unlike Israel, our forefathers came to God with a desire to create a place where his glory would dwell forever. The Lord chased after Israel, but America chased after God and now we have his attention for an eternity. The heart of America was once like that of David when he desired to build a temple for the Lord. Early Americans desired to build a nation to honor God. We may not have been consistent in our efforts to honor him, but God still maintains the Mayflower covenant with America, in addition to his covenant of promise to all believers around the world. What God is seeking is a people would honor the things that he honors according Isaiah 58:7. Americans can be so involved with church that they forget the reason Jesus came. Yes it was to seek and save the lost, but he also told us feed the hungry, clothed the naked, care for the sick, the prisoner and stranger amongst us.

The Lord needs us. There is nothing happening in the world around us, that God has not foreseen and planned for. We only need to seek God in earnest and fervent prayer to find the solutions. Then we must execute God's plan only. This will allow the supernatural power of God to overtake the enemy and overturn the destruction in the earth. The whole earth is groaning for the manifestation of the Sons of God. They want us to come forth, execute the vision and relieve this world of all its pain and suffering. Beloved, I urge you to obey God. Then watch him miraculously move upon the people of the earth with all his goodness and prosperity. Now that's tremendous power beyond anything we could ever do on our own. These are the signs and wonders that follow the word of God if we obey him. This is honest to goodness faith; the God kind of faith that has been deposited as treasure in these earthen vessels of ours; a faith that is destined to change the world!

Key Scripture References

Psalm 24:1
The earth is the Lord's and the fullness thereof, the world and they that dwell there in.

Psalm 2:8
Ask of me, and I shall give you the heathen for your inheritance, and the uttermost parts of the earth for your possession.

Romans 8:16-17
The Spirit itself bears witness with our spirit, that we are the children of God: And if children, then heirs; Heirs of God, and joint-heirs with Christ.

Hebrews 11:6
Without faith it is impossible to please Him. He that comes to God must believe that he is, and that he is a rewarder of those who diligently seek him.

ABOUT THE AUTHOR

In 1997, the Lord commissioned Ms. Matthews to teach about the King-dom of God in order to prepare his people for a spiritual, economic and political paradigm shift in America. *American Heritage Prophecy Series* as presented by EPIC Books and Cafe takes a prophetic look at God's covenant operating within the American culture. It also serves as the follow up to her book entitled, *American Heritage 101*, *A Mini Course on American Values Past, Present and Future*. These and other of her books are available worldwide in both digital and print formats.

BIBLIOGRAPHY

Copeland, Kenneth; Roberts, Oral; Roberts, Richard. *The Wake-Up Call*. Fort Worth: Kenneth Copeland Publications, 2004.

Matthews, Paula. *The War Journal (1999-2010) Volume I*. Los Angeles: Spirit & Life Publications, 2010.

Matthews, Paula. *The War Journal (1999-2010) Volume II*. Los Angeles: Spirit & Life Publications, 2011.

Matthews, Paula. *American Heritage 101*. Shaker Heights: Spirit & Life Publications[SM], 2012.

The Holy Bible: Authorized King James Version. Nashville: Thomas Nelson, 2003.